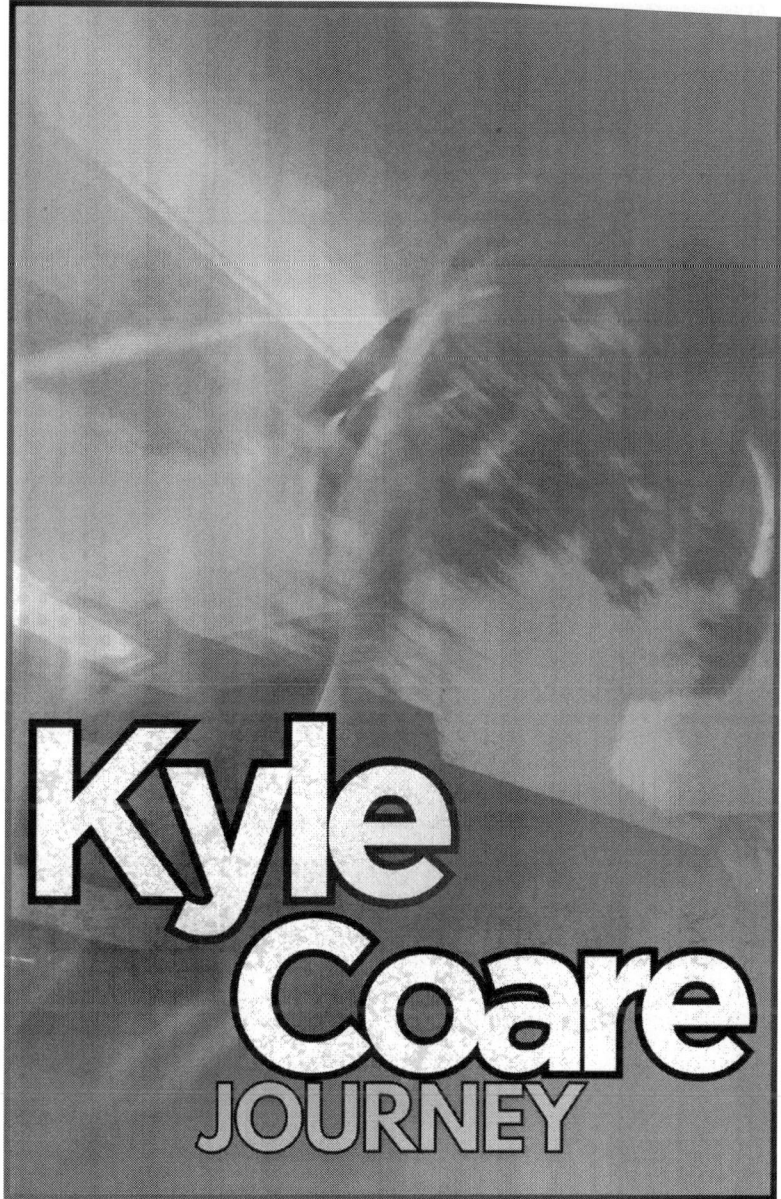

Kyle Coare

JOURNEY

Journey

Kyle Coare

Other works by Kyle Coare.

Poetry

Prisoner of the mind
Prisoner of the heart
The night watchman*
Seasons*
Lone wolf*
Headfirst into the storm*
In shadows**
Torn pages: Scraps of midnight*
Endless nightmares**
Carpe noctem*
Poetic outlaw**
Tales from the 44A**
Stations**

Short Stories

Midnight tales 1: Arty's tale**

Non-Fiction

A brief history of video games*

All available from Amazon
in both Paperback and Kindle editions
*Also available in Hardback
** Also available as Audible Audiobook

Acknowledgements

Since I started this trilogy of books, my health has been gradually declining until I ended up needing a lengthy spell in hospital and quite a few lifestyle changes, So, I really want to share my love with my family, Mum, who visited me so often whilst I was in hospital, even though it was a real struggle for her, and for being here and supporting me through the life changes, and of course my work. Damon & Lucy, Logan, Maisy, Ryan & Elli, Amber. Each one of you has made me smile, gave love when needed, or space when I'm battling with my anxiety.

The poetry community. You are absolutely brilliant incredible people, you always blow my mind with your words and the ways you think, and how everyone is so loving and supportive. One of the main things I missed when ill was being able to get to shows, and to spend a bit of time around that magical energy.

To my get mouthy family, every month we see new faces, and we welcome them in, giving a place to share their words with us. It always amazes me the quality of poets that take our little basement stage, and every single one of you is improving by leaps every month. This brings me so much warmth.

Some-Antics and Sammy, without your guidance and advice I wouldn't be doing what I am now. You gave me the belief that I can do any of this stuff if I put my mind to it. Our little chats really inspire me, the collective events are a place for me to be a little sillier, though some poems in these books have had their first seeds planted there.

Ellie, this year has really showed me not just how great a poet you are, but also that you are a brilliant person. I absolutely love talking with you about life and poetry, we always have so much to say. Now stop reading this and get your book finished, it will be brilliant. Look forward to seeing you again soon.

Jazmine, you are a great friend, and I'm so glad you have started your own poetry night. You are a natural fit for it. I love how much we inspire so much work out of each other, just by talking about general day to day stuff. I am really looking forward to seeing your work evolve and grow, you have such a good solid base that it will be stunning.

Sharena, I was so lucky that we sort of drifted into each other's paths over on Instagram, it has been really nice to share this part of the journey with you. Your work is so inspirational, from the poetry to the different events you put together, and I'm honoured to be able to help with these when my skills are needed.

A huge thank you to anyone that works for the NHS you all do such amazing things; you are true heroes.

The names could go on, but I only have a page.

So, one final thank you, to every single person that reads my work, watches my videos etc. It means the world to me.

Peace, Love & Poetry.

Introduction

This book has had a lot of ups and downs along the road,
things were moving along fairly smoothly but then a series
of health issues laid me up in a variety of hospital beds.
The lengthiest spell was a month in hospital,
with one of my lungs being compressed by a lot of fluid.
I was inserted with a chest drain,
which proceeded to empty my lung a little too quickly,
giving me a collapsed lung. Unable to breath
until they refilled me with some much-needed oxygen.
About 12 years ago I had a shunt put in down my jugular and into an artery
helping my blood flow correctly.
Whilst doing checks they found that this was clotted
and wasn't working, so needed to perform some surgical wizardry,
basically, cutting a hole in the artery in my neck,
and shoving a series of wires down to try to dislodge the clot.
This didn't quite work so plan c or d
was to put a balloon down there and inflate it
cutting around the edges.
Now this was one of the most painful things I've ever had done,
imagine walking barefoot into a room,
with one foot stepping on a Lego,
whilst the other steps on an upturned plug,
causing you to jolt and repeatedly stub your toe.
It was kind of like that but a million times worse,
but at the end of it I had a working shunt again.
Over the month I was in the staff were amazing,
kind, respectful and caring.
You really could not ask too much of them,
they really helped during the dark scary lonely nights.
So, this book is the final part of my "Travels with pen" trilogy
It will cover lots of aspects of life.
Whereas the two previous books
were mostly about actual journeys,
this one is more focused on the journey of life
and the mind. Hope you enjoy my work.

Peace, Love & Poetry
Kyle

Seedling to a sapling

Born from darkness
into the perplexing,
blinding light.
Blinking back tears
from curious eyes.
Unaccustomed
to the fierce sight
of a ferocious burning sun,
the fire it ignites. The strange way
exotic views cover unfamiliar skies.

First pangs of air
inflate desperate lungs,
oxygen runs through
bloodstream riverways.
Feeding organs
the blessed energy needed
to help our bodies run.
The cogs in the mind
start to turn, clockwork thoughts
tick along, not yet fully formed
just whispered echoes,
a lilting windchime song.

The journey only just begun,
a seedling of meaning
planted in the midday sun
to grow into a sapling.
One day you'll be a tree
full of the wisdom of time,
wise enough to see
that this is all part
of life's amazing journey.

Your bark
will hold
onto stories,
each mark on
weatherbeaten
woody skin,
a moment of history,
a memento of yesterday.
A reminder of loves
little victories.

Leaves will be nourished,
amongst them
songbirds will flourish,
inspiring you to become
your own tree, deep in a forest
of identical clone mimicry,
of what other trees
think a tree should be.

You will stand alone,
proud and tall.
Your story never set in stone,
more like how waterways
ripple with the ebbs and flows.
There will be winter downfalls,
when the chill of snow
makes if feel like everything
is slowing to a crawl,
but then the spring sun
will arrive, thawing it all.

The humble pen

It can solve equations,
unite and divide nations.
Against all expectation it can
bring home some hope and elation.
It can talk of love, but also hurt and deflation,
it will sometimes share words you fear to speak
other times, words that narrate new foundations

It can create the worlds
your eyes have sought for so long to see.
It can sketch out your dreams,
or draw on your inspiration,
creating stretched out new scenes.
It can give music meaning,
the message it needs to speak.
In songs it can make us dance,
feeling the universe joining our feet.
Leaving us entranced when everything else
is leaving you feeling bleak.

The humble pen, a magical item.
It seems like nothing,
but combine it with a mind that's open,
and a notepad,
paper mildly glowing under candlelight glare,
and it's a magic wand casting spells in the air.
Illuminating the hidden messages
of the untold storyline strands
that the universe hides
somewhere in the everlasting sands
with just a flick of her hands.

.

It can turn wrongs right,
inspire lives to take
pathways into light,
instead of seeking solace
in the darkest nights.
It can give smiles,
laughter, joy and more.
It can highlight our strengths.
Help us to repair our flawed thoughts.
When knocked down on the floor,
it can fill us with strength
to climb right back up.
The humble pen could stop any war,
with just a squiggled line.
Who could ask for more?

The humble pen could bring peace,
underlined, signed and italicised.
We could all be free.
The humble pen
could feed a million,
if it was held by different men.
The humble pen will always keep
our stories safe for when we need to re-read.
It will listen like our best friend,
it will know of the love
that sits in the hearts of men,
and it will help them
to find the strength to share
that love with everyone.

Train of thought

I hear
the onslaught,
hail against
the buckling tin roof
of my train of thought.
It crawls slowly
along overgrown tracks,
like a serpent slithering
through memory stacks,
long believed
abandoned patches,
hidden by leaves
where decimated forests
have silently grown back.
Reclaiming their lands,
however damaged and cracked.

I hear the scrape of sand
blasting the carriages clean.
Sandpaper dreams clear my mind
and on this train that I've caught,
the chain of thought
is picking up speed.
Trying to avoid
the grains of sand that tickle
times trickling hours to sleep.

I feel I'm going off track,
I've followed this path for so long
it would be pointless turning back.
The world behind would feel so wrong,
so, I keep following along. Knowing
that there is always darkness ahead,
but sensing that the light in the tunnel,
is not a call to my death bed,
but a firm promise
of a brighter future instead.

Rest stop,
empty train-station
coffee shop.
A hot spot
of aroma and scent.
I purchase a sizzling platter
of food for thought.
Tempting my mind
to climb down
from the train to see
what I've bought.
Overwrought from
the short circuit in my mind,
but my growling stomach
aches for more inspiration
on which to dine.

A new day

The sun blinked back
tears of night-time.
Took one solitary look
at the day ahead,
rolled over in her bed.
Said to herself.

*"Not today. No one notices
the work I do anyway."*

She closed drained, tired eyes.
Fiery tear trickling from the side.
A weird light brewed over the countryside.

The stars looked on in shock,
and just a hint of delight,
this hadn't happened before,
but it will serve those humans right.
Gossip spread amongst
the twinkling crowd,
soon replaced by yawns
as they too were tired
to stand around.
They needed their beds
to rest their sharp, pointed heads.

"Whatever will we do"

The north star said,
always the leader,
at least in his own head.

*"If we turn in, then the universe
will go dark. Even the moon
isn't looking herself.* It's so cold and stark"

The luna crown placed head down,
halo removed, her glow now a light frown.
How can she soothe when she aches
so much herself?
Too saddened to share a smile,
all she wants is to flee behind the clouds.

The world stopped suddenly.
People looked up.
Confusion became concern,
twirling headfirst into fear.
In the darkness, the guns fell silent.
They could finally hear!
In the weird light people didn't fight,
they sought out those in need of help,
offered respite from the coldness of night.
They spoke to strangers.
In the darkness they ignored the walls of difference
that had been built up
through years of ignorance and blind indifference,
now instead, they embraced their existence.

The sun looked on,
sad eyes started to sparkle.
For so long she had sat
and witnessed the human debacle.
Hatred spread like butter
slathered on toast,
anger brewed
like a bubbling kettle,
poured over beans
that had been left to roast,
but this one unique day,
none of the anger occurred,
they just shared breakfast,
as the sun lit up the sky.

A rose by the lakeside

Across those murky depths, I wept,
tears dropped like weights of lead.
They kept on flowing even as I slept.
In ripples upon the deep dark depths
I saw my face, flushed red with regret,
in circumspect moments of self-neglect,
I swam in those lakes of tears that I had left.

My dreams became unstuck,
like a gown of sleep slipping
into the moonstruck murky depths.
Those dingy waters, so dark and deep,
I dredged through these fluid thoughts
that wilfully creep through my head whilst
in sleep my tears still wept.
Dreams derelict.
Pain rippling
the surface
as my body
slept through
the rain.

To find
a rose
being swept
along the
water's edge.

That rose,
a reminder of love.
Arrows flew inside
but my heart arose,
to fly so high above.
It beat a rhythm,
to every lonely heart.

Don't feel alone.
It drummed.

There is someone
just waiting
for the right time
to come and blow
the grim air apart.

I listened,
and realised,
to my surprise
the tears had started
to dry from my eyes.
So, like my heart
my hope did rise,
singing in sweet,
improvised lullabies.
Love will arrive,
when time decides,
don't fear the way
that future roads may lie.

Known these tides

I've known these tides.
We flowed together,
side by side
for aeons at a time.
We know each other,
almost intimately.
She has held me
as I waved time away.
Then brought me back
when I was all lost at sea.

I have known these winds.
We've blown together frequently,
I've flown her skies
as she has encircled me.
Protectively watching over me
with caring eyes.
She has carried me
when I'm a dead weight
on feet of clay.
She's pushed me o greater heights.
She's torn apart clouds
so, I can see the light of day,
and she has kept them clear
so, I see stars at night
twinkling away.

And in thunderous times,
when the wind chimes,
wild, she has always gone
that extra mile.
Making sure the downpour
doesn't sour her glowing smile.
Protecting her own self,
so that she has enough strength
to share with everyone else.

I've walked this grass,
its green wonderland carpet.
A woodland clearing,
a carousel of dreams.
I've walked her moonbeams.
Her majestic parapet
keeping me safely in step.
I've visited her dreams,
and she doesn't even
know my name yet.
I'm just someone that visits
her umbrella skies
whenever I can.

A light touch

Stars shine within her eyes,
a light touch
making everything feel alright,
and if a comet appeared
in our night skies for just a blink,
before crashed into earth,
bringing the rubble
of an apocalyptic aftermath,
as continents sink.
I'd still only see those lights shining bright.
You could say I'm a troubled, delusional guy.
It's true that she doesn't contain
a ball of nuclear fusion inside,
but I swear it's not illusional.
Her love is star sized.

And if our tides were sent askew,
drowning the cities,
streets and avenues.
I'd still feel her,
soothing my own storms.
Calming my boat
so, I can still sail on.
You may call me irrational,
playing with make belief.
But I know the relief she brings
when she smiles.
It's behind those tantalising eyes.
I've felt the tides within me
become mirror reflective glass,
and this is no tale of fantasy,
or story written in the bygone past.

She holds the seasons
in her lips.
In summery she brings passion,
springs a rebirth in wintery cold hearts,
and revitalises those autumn sighs
when darkness starts to slip,
but it's in her eyes
that the universe
really shines out.

People may call me
a dreamer, fantasist.
I prefer romanticist.
I know the way forever feels
when it is kissed
by eternities warming lips.

And like a river
these thoughts
keep flowing.
Like breathing
they just appear.
Never cease moving me to tears,
even when the banks are eroded
and someone has dammed the way.
There are no words to describe
the sway her waters hold over me.

She smiles
and I'm just clouds
in the air, floating.
Her magic is always there
and I'll keep it close to me
every single day.

Kyle Coare

Head down

Head down.
Avoid contact of the eye,
a soundless pact with the sky.
I'll keep my gaze on the ground,
if you promise
to protect from on high.
Keep to yourself. Voice, silent.
On this side of town
things can quickly turn violent.
Screams can become sad sighs.

The smell of weed clings to the air,
growing like a vine on a trellis.
It persists, climbing
into every crack it can find.
Scratching itself into
the dense atmosphere.

Top off, tattooed bod,
walks in the cold chill air.
"Who wants some? Come on
I'll take on everyone."
Screeched from the top
of his scarred lungs.
Where are the plod?
White lines stretched out
somewhere behind,
but that thin blue one
is seemingly long gone.

Don't look. Don't glance up.
Just watch the cracked paving underfoot.
Keep to yourself. Head lowered.
On this side of town, always walk forward.
Don't look around.
There is always someone
ready to put you down.
Your grave is already dug,
shallow, somewhere
in the hallowed mud.

Car screeches past,
zipping around corners,
weaving down invisible roads.
Bounding over speed humps,
before they come to a halt on a path.
Fist bumps as they bolt
into the darkness of night.
No police in sight.

Streetlights click off.
Cash over lives.
A gang member runs,
one lay screaming out.
A glint in the moonlight.
Blade, red and bright.
Just another victim
of these streets,
on another frosty night.

Discarded can

Sat in my own shadow
but I don't recognise
his motions.
My emotions too frail
to stop these oceans.

I feel my own shade keeping
the sunshine at bay.
Is it so wrong to want
to feel the love
of a summer day?

I feel the spiral whirlpool
of my own thoughts,
twirling me into a world
somewhere away from here.
I feel the pull taking me
to that place of fear.

It is dark.
So dark.

In here, the lights don't work.
In the distance,
wretched howls, angry growls,
and untamed barks.

But I see nothing.

Just the blurred outline
of the dregs of my heart,
bleeding out my last ebbing fires.
As they drift slowly away
into the night.

In here the sparks of insight
are blighted by demons,
clasping them tight,
dulling their light before
they have had a chance
to shine, inspire or delight.

Sound wails
through this failing
tornado mind,
too many choices
I flail inside.
The braying wind
intoning a raucous chorus
of ill-timed cacophonous noises.
Somewhere deep inside
The shouting gets louder and louder,
this bawling shrieking herd,
warbling for their voices to be heard.

They screech,
a squeal
piercing through my feelings,
squeezing out the last drops
of kindness they find.
Until I sit empty.
A discarded can
kicked along
the roadside again.
To join the mountain of rubbish
that has piled into
the alleyway at the end.

Bookmarked pages

I leave a bookmark dangling over
the precipice of the page,
where my smile first wavered,
then briskly walked away.
Left to fade into the distance,
without any last words to say,
not even a wave, just turned on its heels
and disappeared into the shade.
Now it only ever returns… Infrequently.
A flying visit over stale biscuits and cold tea,
before its away again. No fanfare or symphony,
nor sympathy. Just another memory of a different day.

I have corners folded on lovelorn streets.
Moments of life where bird tweets
out sung the wretched grind
and that clanging hum
that smothered my mind.
The changes of seasons,
when winter turned to icing sugar dreams,
a new love breaking the surface
into joy that starts to spring,
the summer where the blossoms
fade, swaying in the heat haze rising.

In the margins I have scrawled out messages,
the meanings of some lost to the decades,
the meanings of others faded with time,
like a photograph left unshaded in sunnier climes,
but some messages bring out the moments
when life was divine. Full of meaning,
like the way salt enhances taste,
the scrawled handwriting scratched across the page,
enhances the feelings that live within.

The feelings these memories bring
are like a lush green field on a summer day,
butterflies providing acrobatic displays,
bees buzzing peacefully.
Animals running. Children at play.
Short poems I've found
in my minds frail linings,
and had to write them down
as fast as lightning,
before they take off
like clouds and go flying.

There are blackened seascapes,
smeared, flecked
with tissue paper residue,
from the ink blot mistakes,
where I sought escape from the view,
knocking the ink pot over the page.
Doodles dance across the edges,
twirling over
highlighter marked passages,
reversed sentences
seeping through the thinning
membrane of reality,
where my words imagine the future,
until I find a better way to write.

Halfway through,
the pages become clean and new,
like fresh linen. Untouched, undisturbed.
A blanket of snow
with no footprints, no pollutants.
Just an open canvas for our futures
to come to life and be set free,
to paint themselves however they wish
their futures to be.

By life's open fire

Unwrapped
that into
which
we
had wound
around ourselves.
We had bound
the night
like a bandage
so tight.

Through
the long night,
we talked, laughed
cried and
worked it all
out.

You see
that's what poetry...
No wait... That's what life
is all about.
Finding our
stories deep inside
and pulling them
out into the light.
Sharing them out,
like a meal, a feast.
Sating our hunger,
stopping us feeding
on neglect and lack of self-belief.

We give
and we take.
We share what
we make.
We talk,
we laugh,
we cry,
we fight.
We find meaning,
we resolve,
finding answers
to that big question, why.
Then we hug and retire,
play games
as we perspire
by life's open fire.

And as the evening
is drawing,
we play charades
with our lives.
Trying to squeeze
our thoughts and feelings
into a quick simple mime.
Hearty meals of life
condensed to mere
soundless soundbites.
But when the day ends
we play games
by life's open flames,
finding our stories
again and again,
igniting intense fires
to bring to life
our minds burning pyres.

Daisy chain

I hear you when
the songbird speaks,
just before it sings out
its lonely tweet.
Seedling thoughts
spreading from
its fledgling beak.
I hear you
in the breath
it breathes.
Deeply inhaling
then releasing love
into the air above
where it floats away
like straying leaves.

You are the irregular
rainbows that appear
near the water's edge,
like a smiling mirror
greeting the day.
You are the first drops
of snow on a winter's tale.
The oceans I pray to sail.
The beautiful falling leaf
that flows away gently upon
the billowing wind sway.
The colours that stay
etched to the eye,
like a carved name
chiselled upon
the bark of time,
and I want
our two names entwined,
like roots beneath
this forest of mine.

You laid a daisy chain
of expression. A tantalising
taste of heaven, lightly binding
soft gentle ribbons to my grains
of introspection. I started to feel
the ground swelling. A flourishing
ocean of words flowering forth.
a chorus of birds. A pull deep
to the core. You spoke from
the earth, from the very
depths underfoot.
You spoke from the skies
a message of love.
You spoke in the tastes
of a summer fruit cup.
You spoke to me
and I drank it all down
in a single gulp.

I feel you in the warm sun,
a golden cuddle given form
in forged sun-kissed memories.
I feel you in the dance
of the early dawn,
and in the twilight
embrace when night-time falls.
I feel you pushing me on,
like a supportive hand
upon my shoulder
guiding towards
the right horizon.
Where the future is bright
and the sun is bolder.

Kyle Coare

A blanket peace

I let stillness
fall over me,
a blanket peace,
coating
the noise I've
been hearing.

A moment of tranquillity
in the rumble of fear
I feel getting near.
An instance of hope
in this downward
dragging existence
that I'm constantly reliving.

I listen to the grass
reaching out
into the warm breeze.
As if it can touch
the delicate breath
as it leaves moistened lips
and lightly teases,
aiming to please.

I see the shimmer
of summer sunlight
reflecting
in shivering leaves.
I hear the tree bark
creak
like aching joints
resting into place.
I see the clouds
slow their pace.

I feel light.
flowing
through the air,
gently brushing,
sharing its loving
warmth everywhere.

Calming air forms
around me,
like a long soak
in a deep warm
bubble bath,
I feel I'm afloat.
Fragrances rising
like the relieving motion
of an ocean bound boat.
Nature's undying love.
The fluid serenity.

A light drizzle

Don't get me wrong…
I love rainy days.
There is nothing better
than sitting in a warm study,
scalding steam from your hot cocoa,
rises across reminiscent eyes.
Misting the view, to give a foggy screen
to see your memories through.
Watching lightning ripping a hole
through the storm clouds
amassed across the skies.
Dark grey mountains of hate,
no silver shimmery linings
or bright beaming sunrays in sight.
But there is magic at play
when those powerful forces get their way.

I love the way
lightning tips the balance
from night to day, from dark to light
then back again in the blink of an eye,
like a child flicking the light switch.
On and off. On and off.
The way the flowers sway,
looking for cover, then realising they
are stuck in place,
dripping from their petal umbrellas.
But this isn't that sort of rain.
This is liquid hate. It brings pain,
in trickles. It can seem so innocuous,
almost like paper cuts.
It starts off feeling like tickles.
But before you realise it...

It is eating away
at your sinewy flesh.
Devouring your
dwindling will to live.

A downpour
that eyes can barely see,
it's so sneaky,
almost just misty.
But the air is full
of this fluid misery.
It deceives you into thinking
it's just a fine rain drizzle,
before dousing you,
in what can only be
described as hellfire sizzle.

In this hellish downpour
the combined oceans soar
overhead. Riverbeds lay naked,
seas sit emptied, as it all seems
to be flooding directly overhead,
and then directly into your face.
A cold embrace
with an angry mace.
Slumped like
a drowned rat,
now floating lifeless
on the surface.
Flowers drowning,
but still, it doesn't cease.
Bloated flora becomes obese,
they can't take much more.

The sound of stems
creaking in the breeze.

Upon journeys with pen

Upon journeys
with pen,
notepad glistening.
I listened to my
journals sing.
My feet
merely walking,
but there was a bit of a swing
to the way I was almost floating.
I saw sights,
mind invigorated by the bright insights.
Nightlights reignited
love that lived inside,
locked tight,
but it had begun to
wriggle...

Free.

Upon journeys with pen
I saw galaxies colliding.
Unsoiled worlds
hidden in the streaks
of cosmic lightning.
I left the stuttering
street lighting
and ventured
into the fiction of stars.
The fractured cosmos.
A mirror pane, smashed,
a fraction away from ours.

Upon journeys with pen,
my notepad bristling.
Words erupted
like confetti dreams.
Party poppers
of word streams
bursting from
the worn-out seams.
I listened to my fantasies
as they gasped out futures.
Were these futures
painted for me?
Or worlds
I just wished to be?

Upon journeys
with pen,
I sought answers
to questions
long caught in my throat,
but the more I wrote,
the more questions I evoked.
Provoking my mind
to dig deeper.
To get to the hidden treasure
buried under that secluded beachside,
but what if there is no treasure to find?
Then I'll have
all of my adventures
still to write.

On the edge of a melody

As I sit in this
delusional mimicry
of happiness,
a mask of lies,
there to hide that inside
I'm feeling
inconsequential.

See, my shell of illusion
is failing me,
and I'm showing the truth,
in the
uncoordinated
sadness
that encircles,
like a whirlpool
sucking in the sea.

A part of me
is tied to a dream.
Par for the course it seems,
and that dream
can never be reality,
it's a fallacy,
built of hope and
stale old star dust,
and this big, old,
frail lungful of love
that I breathe.
But alas, it's not enough
to just believe.

So, I hold out a hand.
Come and meet with me
where the dream
parts ways with reality.
Let us just sit in that world
for a day,
I'll sleep away
the hurt,
if you'll dream
with me today.

Let this world of mine
encircle you
and give to you
all the love
I have stored inside.
So that you
can spread it wide,
wherever your wings
can fly.

See I'm floating
precisely
where I always
find myself.
Somewhere out to sea.
The waves speaking to me,
greeting me. My feelings
precariously perched
on the edge
of a strummed gentle
melody. Telling me
that love will
hear my song
eventually.

Jewel on the tide

A vision
of beauty,
on these cold,
lonely nights.
When the shadows
dare to play
and dirty gremlins
put up a fight.

Her swaying
lavish hair,
orange in the moonlight glisten,
worn tied back, a sight
like a suit of sunlight,
a sunflower
in a field of thorns,
its majestic power
skulking
through storms,
like a fox
creeping by
to get back
to its lair.

Her smile
as golden
as earth's
mightiest treasures.
The burden of pressure
evaporated from sight.
All I could witness,
the pleasure
of this jewel
on the tide.

Her glorious eyes.
So many questions
I could ask them.
I'm taking
a running jump
at the lake
of answers,
and I dive headfirst in.
Feeling
the waters
break around me,
the
waves
take me,
to the banks
on the other side.
To be beside
the jewel
on the tide.

Under
luxurious skies,
my gaze
would never rise
above the horizon.
For to glance away
would be enough to drain me
of so much warmth,
that I'd freeze internally.

Kyle Coare

The silence of the hour

I find a lot of poets
are tied to the moon,
the nightly cycle
of planets circling
in solitude.
The chimes of midnight
seem to suit our moods.
During the lateness of the hour,
when life slows down,
there is a unique power,
the air gets charged
with a new attitude,
and calmness grows over us
like a blanket of flowers.

Rarely a car will drive across town,
merely solitary taxis
crossing the yawning chasm,
the darkness of time.
Betraying
the silence of the hour,
then they are forgotten
in a single blink of the eye,
but barely any sound
pierces our contemplation.
Nothing can stir
the spinning waters
of our deep reflection
the introspection that sits
in every rippling wave
nothing can swirl
our imagination away.

We welcome the solitude, the bliss,
the way words kiss our lips
landing with a fizz.
We have our own unique way
of winding the hands
of the clock around,
until they find the right groove,
like a ticking record player,
begging us to move.

The late-night hours,
darkness freckled with light,
speckles of worlds we can explore,
when we open our mind doors wide.
Moonbeams show us
the skyward passageways to fly
until we find worlds of golden shores,
where words saturate the night.

Words and letters, mystical symbols
imagery from somewhere
complex but simple,
They rain down
like the most refreshing shower.
Imbuing us with words
of the greatest power.
Inspiring us to witness the subtleness,
of the miniscule,
whilst looking over the vast
galactic pool
so full of forevers
that we can feel and touch,
and as we stand by that waterside
we can swirl our own
stories into the tide, creating space inside
for whole new tales to reside.

Forgive my ghosts

As the train sidles closer
to the end of the line,
and the clock idles towards
the looming, final seconds of time.
I forgive my ghosts
for the torment.
Their scares were only meant
as lessons. Sent to aid me.
To help me prepare,
and I apologise in return, for the times
I've given those same ghosts a fright.
When I've been wide awake,
crying lakes, when they appear
in the middle of the night.

The clock hopefully has a few more spins.
The roulette wheel
of time, for all of its sins,
still in its infancy,
and I still hold all of my chips,
even if they are burning holes in my fingertips.
I still have so much more to learn
from relationships. To give up
would be a titanic waste of life.
I have an overflowing heart of love
to give to all, but whenever I'm flying high,
and my mind starts going too fast,
time speeding past,
I need darkness to fall.
I still have an army of ghosts
upon whom I can call.
I still have a yearning
to make the most of my life
if I still have any choice at all.

I'll keep on
riding the tracks
wherever these
rolling wheels spin.
I'll live for love.
Not material gain.
I'll go through pain
again, and again.
Of this I'm certain.
But I know it will
ease in the rain,
giving a new lease of life,
to find new stories to release.
On this ghost train
I'll take a journey of reflection,
see the mirror seas,
showing me stories
to paint pictures,
for future witnesses
to decipher
as they please.

Teetering

We let our words sit.
Teetering on the edge of a precipice.
One forceful outward exhale
and they will slip.
But we need to be sure
that what we want to say,
is what we need to say.
That letting those words strip
back the blinds,
won't open
windows onto a blustery day.

So, we hold them back,
just enough that we can see
the ocean spray,
but far enough away
to stop the breeze
from carrying them
into the waves,
or blowing into our face.

We let our words stand.
Alone. Withstanding
gale force winds.
As we ourselves edge
gingerly inlands. Scared
of the ocean swells that could befall
once these words have fell.
We let our words sway
uneasily on the brink, one slip
and they will sink.
To unleash a flood
that will submerge everything,
and then we will be left alone once again.
Floating on driftwood with nothing to say.

So, we hold them back.
Always holding back.
Now too many letters
filling up too many
sentence backpacks.
Too many words straddling
the lines of our notepads.
Whilst lining up even more to join in.
We can't stop these taps from pouring.
We let our words seep out gently,
mere trickles at a time.
If you read intently
you may be able to join the lines,
see the dots being connected.
Our collective thoughts imitating dust,
to hide away thoughts
that could push
our words over that precipice,
and unleash a flood
of pain to wash over us.

Lights of the heart

Starry night.
I mouth to you
unprepared
silent words.
No sound
peppering the air.
No words
disturbing the atoms,
nor breaching the
perfect atmosphere.

Just motions of lips
whispering a kiss,
but you hear,
in those mimes
the undeclared emotions
meant for your ears,
to share my heart,
to cleanse your tears.

Insights into this mind.
Moonlight shines,
illuminating ley lines
that lay on the lazy ground.
Love signs written
into the world
all around,
always leading
like a circular pathway
back to you.

Starry nights echo
a twinkling
bell ringing
symphony.
The lines glow,
rose coloured love.
An epiphany.
Those lines always
moved wherever
the music flowed.
Wherever it took
your feet.
Those lines
would always
follow your heartbeat.

I wonder do you see
the same lines?
The way they stop
at my feet,
as if we were always
destined to meet,
as if these lines
were sung in harmony
to a majestic long written
cosmic signature piece.

Did fate tie the ends so tight
that whichever pathway
we could walk,
would always end up
in that same place,
on that same night.
Somewhere under a starry sky,
watching as the love lights
draw a heart around our silent sighs.

Kyle Coare

Dreaming in poetry

Into those satin-like
sweeping words, I fall.
Blissfully they enthral me,
enchanting me tightly
in their shrouding blanket.
Longingly, I've started to
dream in gold-laced poetry,
it's a little weird at first,
it comes like an explosive burst,
words surround in shrapnel verse,
without warning.

You awaken in a world
full of bounding synonyms
tweeting out a metaphorical flurry,
singing in keys of ambiguous rhythm
to the white fluffy pillows
dancing across larimar skies, windows
open upon a bright summers morning,
where lemon beams awaken your eyes.
Rhymes meandering alongside
verdant verandas of vast countryside.

Your feet begin to disintegrate
into wide-eyed verses, contained inside
refrains of images, fleeting visions
seen before they hide.
propelling you forward,
across the universe's grandest sights.
Words twinkling, bright,
and a thousand glowing suns,
dials not set too high,
so the light won't blind,
just provide a nice shine,
to warm the corners
of your mind.

Body becomes liquid state,
then evaporates into vapour
as it takes to the clouds
tiny pieces of torn up paper.
I'm dreaming in poetry,
it's true.
Raining streams of inky blue
across the parchment ground,
slowly the streams
begin to spread around.
Across the paper,
words forming loud.

See,
I'm dreaming
in poetry,
asleep
in its
soft flowing
consistency.
For if I open my eyes,
all I see
is a world aflame.
Burning
with
misery.

Fruit

Strolling through the forest
with my journeyed pen.
Searching this darkened
corner of my mind again,
for a tree that looks ready
to provide some fruit for me.
The fruit needs to be juicy
so I can shake it free, to let it flow
across my lips, down to my blistered throat
and deep into the core of me.
My charred heart
barely beating in scarred agony.
My burning throat. Parched,
dry as a bone
sat in the desert heat.
It needs to be replenished,
by something sweet.
Relishing the feeling as it cools
my heat seared lips.

Strolling through the forest
with my humble pen,
notepad open
but only empty pages showing.
No fruit could I spy,
so now I search
low and high.
Maybe if I'm quiet,
inspiration
will just walk by.
I need to confess,
I'm craving
some sweetness
to cut through
this bitter taste
that coats my lips.

The fourth wall collapses in front of me,
as I scramble to rebuild, I attest that
the fruit is a metaphor for poetry,
and my brain is almost empty,
needing to be refilled.
My mind sits away somewhere, silent,
except for the weeping sound drifting
across the stale air. The words are hiding
elsewhere now. Deep in the forever seas,
just trying to avoid being seen,
only themselves to please

But wait... Is that a noose hanging
from the nearby tree?
Am I walking into dangerous territory,
or are the branches just taunting me?
By talking about writing my poetry,
am I angering the words within?
Like a magician explaining his tricks,
or an author spoiling the ending to his own story.

If I entertain these thoughts,
will my voice fail me?
Will I clog up my throat?
The skin of some rotten fruit,
lodged deep inside of me,
jagged barbs hanging on tightly.
What if my well ceases to refill?
How will I be able to stay healthy?
Is this the tree of mental blockage?
The one that bears the most tempting fruit,
but when you take a bite, it devours you internally,
sapping your energy and mentally entrapping you.
Leaving your mind forever empty,
just staring at the moon.

World of howevers

I found peace
at the edge of forever,
I looked
into the distance
and saw that there
was a world
of howevers. Buried treasures.
Maybes, sat beside
definitelys.
Possibilities
stretched away
independently into infinity.

Undeniability
dropped like rain,
with no hostility,
just to help grow,
the flowers of possibility.
I witnessed
the spanning jaws
that never clamped shut.
The open doors which
could sometimes
provide a shortcut.
The wide-open spaces,
which were yet to be
traipsed upon by human foot,
or the pages that were not yet
tarnished with inky soot.

And I felt
a buzz,
like a sprinkler
showering
a live wire.
My mind,
alive,
neurons
on fire.
I was
inspired.
I had found
new desire
to forever
follow
the path,
whatever
outcome
could
transpire.

A fallen acorn

A lone acorn drops
almost silently,
but the squirrel
runs towards the sound.
Never stops.
He feels the vibrations,
knows the sensations
like sonar to find the tree.

The squirrel
carries away
his treasure.
Like a pirate
he buries it for later,
for those times
when the weather
is dire
and hibernation
is his one pleasure.
During these times
an acorn can be
as warming as an open fire.

As the
snows fall
the squirrel
doesn't come to call.
His stock of acorns
will keep him going
until the springtime thaw.
So, the acorn sits
in the dark all alone,
but inside a spark
starts to glow.

The acorn bursts free,
a sapling taking
his first breath
of nature's beauty.
Slowly
limbs start to grow,
his roots stretch
all across this hallow.
Baby leaves
begin to blow,
branches reach out
stretching out the aches
from his time down below.

Long years pass.
An oak tree stands
where the acorn was cast.
Strong as the blowing winds
carrying away thoughts of the past.

A lone acorn drops
almost silently.
A squirrel sneaks in
to grab his feast.
The cycle repeats,
time duplicates
so breathtakingly
its beauty.

In amongst the butterflies

In amongst
the butterflies,
on the weary side
of a tired mind.
Slowly ambling up the
stone staircase, lined
with feather-full,
fluffy pillows.
White cloudy skies
smoothly glide
behind drowsy blue eyes.
To rest the ache inside, I climb.

In amongst
the swirling thermals,
I sway my way,
gently step by slow step,
no need to rush,
just taking in each lungful
of citrus fresh breath,
and letting it go again
as onwards I push.
I hear the sound of my bed
singing to me, in the wispy words
of a mystic melody.

Where the songbirds
tweet a soft refrain,
welcoming the night-time
to whisk the day away.
They sing a gentle lullaby
to put my pain to sleep.
As I languidly start to count
calmly bounding imaginary sheep.

I slowly dawdle
to the peaceful place,
my own little private
pocket of space,
just outside
the Milky Way,
across the galactic
waterways,
where cosmic waterlilies
give the
amphibious aliens
a place to play,
whilst I pull up
my celestial duvet
to rest my eyes
for the day.

Time waves farewell

Time rolls forward
in ever moving waves.
Agitated waters
pulled by the moons seductive rays.
We ride the flowing tides
like a boat in a monsoon.
Never sure of where we are going,
or if we will reach there soon.
What may we find, we are too blinded
by the light cascading
through the crystal rain and spray
to be able to imagine the wonders at play.

We pass our days
endlessly wanting
to be something more,
on some distant shore,
never noticing
the wonders that sit just
outside our unlocked doors.

We pray to be older, wiser,
without noticing that one moment
you are twenty with the world at your feet,
the next retirement edges closer,
beckoning you in with fingers that creak.
This journey is so brief,
yet we seek to waste so much
just searching for instant relief
or a fountain of youth,
it's all make belief.
A faked relief, to escape
from the inescapable hands that sweep
inevitably across the shrinking clock face
at an ever-increasing speed.

We forget the things
that make us
unique.
Our imaginations
raise us
above birds
that tweet.
Our artistry
sets our stories free.
We are
no longer hunters
seeking sustenance,
we have
a world
of abundance,
but we ignore
all of the little things
sitting at our feet.

Torn page yesterdays

My thoughts run rampant,
a herd of untamed words
all seeking solace, their place
in the amber tinged wild woods
of a marigold mirage.
Where ambrosia dreams flow
like custard rivers of fantasy.
They see the yellow sky
adorned with star anise sunlight,
a spiralling spinning sight.
A majestic love story
told upon the intangible highs
of the glowing star light
that I carry forever by my side.

Apprehension heeds
no home within this world,
with its dripping liquid sunbeams,
like paint of the finest gold
forming pools to coat
your wildest dreams.

In the shimmering mirage,
I'm torn page yesterdays.
I see an overlay of grey.
Faded strains
of angry words,
mocking birds swarm overhead,
singing their songs
in violent eruptions,
to make me wish for death.
I take a lungful,
a deep breath,
but all I taste
is bittersweet corruption.

I shake my head
with persistence,
like a child trapped
in a nightmare,
the terror of being
aware of the monsters
but unable
to escape their lair.
Saying no more
to this strained existence
playing
in 3d stereoscopic imagery,
I sprinkle my mind
with colourful confetti memories.
To remind myself
that this instance of time
is no longer reality,
and my world is so much clearer
on the other side of this dream.

Kyle Coare

Sounds at sea

Invigorating temperate nights
should hold us close,
grip us tight.
Darkness could wrap itself
like a bandage to keep
our hurt from flowing out,
but we are trapped by life's
unkind threads, placing us
in the wrong neighbourhoods.
Our playpens stand
across wide open oceans,
we have no boats
and we cannot swim.

Set us free,
we chant
to the moonlight
illuminating
our streets.
We wish
to feel the night,
like the tide
lapping thirstily
at our burning feet.
The urge to move,
so primal,
fiercely
trying to make
all other thoughts
unravel.
We deserve to be free
of these chains
that shackle.
Placed around
us mistakenly.

Our dance floor, merely feet away
but we are caged perpetually,
on two sides of an aching, crying sea.
An endless chasm of broken hearts piled precariously.
Tears making it overflow more each day.
The moon hangs like a disco light,
taunting us. Let you rhythm out,
it sings in glee.
Dance, feel the tide
splash around your feet,
but I don't want to dance,
not without you in my arms.
Your heart beating through me.

The sounds of the sea
offers music in the gentle sway of waves.
The water starts to rust away
the binds chained around our feet.
The motion, slowly but surely
starts a chain reaction.
The chains feeling friction,
rumbling the locks until they
are crumbling like a cliffside tumbling.

The melody of shells engaging,
twisting and taking shape.
Unwinding years of pain.
Blustery breeze blowing a bass line,
making our hips sway.
We dance the final remnants
of the chains away.
Under the moonlight we float
on dreams of future days,
where we will be forever
dancing in each other's arms,
when the waters direct us
to that dancefloor where perfection lays.

Those wise words

I wish to hear
words whispered
from those
long departed.
I wish to see again,
those smiling eyes,
widely parted,
taking in the scenery.
I wish to see them in full 3D,
not merely
a photograph kept lovingly
framed,
a memory to keep
the stories enflamed.

I wish to hear guidance
reverberating
like a bass sound.
Getting deep inside
until I can feel
the internal pound
of danger every time
it is around.
In the guts and chest,
every dripped word
starts to merge
with the nerves
and bones,
to create
an internal alarm,
to never again feel so alone
and to no longer fall to harm.

I wish to sit with
wise words
that string themselves
around my mind room
like spiderweb
washing lines.
I want the hopes
and dreams,
advice and warnings,
to be pegged tightly,
so that when
the winds of doubt start to blow,
the clothesline spins,
but the emotions merely swing,
they never get lost and unconnected
from the little things.

I want to be able
to pluck them free,
word fruit from
spidery clothesline tree,
so I can hear
your wisdom
and let it sink into me.

I wish to hear words
is that too much to ask?
I love the songbirds singing along,
but in words I'd bask.
Time is too short
for all of life's harsh tasks,
we sometimes
miss the moments
that should always last.

Turn back the clocks

Turning back the clocks,
what could you change
and still be you?
You could remove
a limb or two
and not really
alter the view,
but what would
it take to
really alter you?
Shattering the
mirror of reality,
letting imagination
peer through.

If I went through
that doorway marked
with a crookedly
hanging, shiny, silver two,
instead of just following
the number one passageway through,
would I still be me?
Or a mimic modelled
on an uncanny twisted
untrue reality?
Would I still feel
every twinge,
each tear,
would I still howl
at the nightmares
in despair?

If I turned left at the forest path
sneaking under the branch's grasp,
if I felt the lush wet dew under bare feet,
beside some idyllic waterside retreat,
instead of walking through the debris
filled aftermath field of a world that only cares
about what you have. Would I still be
this weak sapling blowing in the breeze?
Or would my roots have grown differently?
Building me up to be the great oak of which
you speak.

If I'd not been so scared, if I had dared
to do the things for which I cared
instead of giving into fear,
would I still be the person sat here?
Would I have learnt to walk tall
instead of cowering at the bottom of it all?
Would that have set my stall differently?
Or would I have still been me?

Knowing that to be me
took every mistake, every heartbreak,
every tear that fell creating huge tidal waves.
Would my feet have caused earthquakes
shaking the earth's very core?
Of any of this, none of us are sure,
but to regret would be saying that
my life is poor, instead, I'm rich
from all the things I adore.
If I could turn back the clocks, would I?
No, I'd rather
spread my wings
and fly.

Words in your soul

Have you ever listened
to the words
in your soul?
The ones
that bubble
and zing.
The ones
at the very core
of everything.
The ones that often sing,
but sometimes cry
when no one is watching.

There is love
deep under the surface,
a mermaid ready to rise,
splashing through
the waters that window your mind.
She surfaces with purpose,
to point in wonder at our skies.
A silent question burned deep into her eyes.
She can never comprehend,
so completely is she submerged,
that she can never fly,
nor understand the way
a yearning souls can cry.

Have you ever listened to that voice inside?
The noise that whispers when silence herself hides.
The one that sits in a darkened room,
whispering of feeling alone in the gloom.
That voice often sits staring out
over an abstract view.
Imagining the moon it saw
in a dream it once knew.

There is love,
it screams.
It knows it is there,
aching
somewhere between
these twisted,
tangled beams of distorted sunlight.
There is love,
it seems lost,
but it lives
in the twilight,
ready to be found again.
If you are on the right path,
on the right night,
when the moon is shining bright,
it will set the fire alight.
Make songs sing again in pride.
So, in the meantime,
share your heart with the moon,
find words inside that show
how much you care,
and love will find you soon.

Campfire

Under campfire gaze,
almost silent
just the crackle
of the kindling flare,
as eyes glare
at the twinkling stars
of the Milky way.
A blaze enlightens
flames across
countryside hideaways,
reading passages
from paper lantern heart pages,
lighting a pathway
through the dense haze.

Stories emblazoned
in starlight shine,
tales of yore mixed
with fables of mine.
We sat where water
flowed like wine.
Intoxicated on the words.
Meticulous and fine.

Under campfire glare.
The swish
of tempestuous flair,
a glint in your eye,
framed by
that luscious long hair.
My fare paid
by the words I impart.
The destination,
a road to my heart.

Underneath campfire
sanctuary,
the heat,
beating away
any coldness
that formed in me.
The heat in our hearts
pouring liquid words
for all to read.
Molten fires
forming on pages
of history.
Our lives,
our loves
telling the stars
our stories.

Kyle Coare

Wear the night

You wear
the night
better than
the sky herself.
The gown
of purple and blue,
a skyward river flow
draping
the brilliance
of you.
The dazzle
of starlight sequins
could never overthrow
Saturn's halo rings,
illuminating your
own inner glow.

You adorn
the glassy form
of sunlight,
brighter than
a spring dawn campsite.
Firelight embers flicker
more enticing than
a summer morn,
as the temperature
jumps fahrenheit
like a golden fawn
moving with the sunshine
across a grassy lawn.

The way
the lights shape
to your frame,
like you have been
dipped in
the luminous paint
that creates the day.
You are the brush
that enlightens
the page.
The delightful dance,
that sets fire
to the stage
as across your body
the lights play.
I could pray
to see this sight
every single day,
but I'd soon go blind
from the wonderous display.

Dark clouds over the horizon

Surreal morning light
like the sky is tripping out.
Everything feels unreal.
Distorted like drizzle
flowing down a windowpane.
Snaps, crackles and pops
as aerials fizzle, Tv serials ripple
as the rain threatens the day
with an electrical sizzle.

In static,
buzzing atmosphere,
I fear a storm
is brewing.
Something slowly stirring,
as the broth is stewing,
ready for the wind to blow it in.
A strange haunting glow in the air.
Taunting the sun, daring it to appear,
but dark clouds are massing everywhere.

The first drops alight,
as successfully
as the wright brothers
initial test flights,
crashing down to earth
like sparks from a fire,
glistening in the curious light
before they have
a chance to burn any brighter.

The tinkling bell-like sounds,
wind chimes caught
under torrential water onslaught.
Gnomes would run for cover.
Bird homes wobble
in the increasing bluster.
The drumbeat pounding
on bass drum tables.
Sounds shouted down guttering pipes,
drowned out
by powerful thunder strikes.
Neptune makes a primal squall.
A yell to call his armies forward.
invasion now reality,
as the heavy rain ceaselessly falls.

Underneath charged air,
a rousing crescendo.
I hear it, as trees bend, blown
by the gales increasingly
gathering speeds.
Dark clouds growing thicker.
Headache as the storm gets nearer.
I wish to just dance in the downfall,
feel the waters wash away
the hurt of this world.
Feel the charge tingle
through tired skin.
Reinvigorate
my lost feelings.

Astral plane

Mournful sobs
hang timelessly
onto the minute hands of the clock,
spinning slowly, soundlessly.
Sees family, heads bowed.
Looking down
at a plot on the ground.
A blot over the sun.
A dark cloud
leadens the day, he walks away.
Trying to find a safe space
for his soul to lay.

Meanders the dark spaces.
The veiled streets
of the other side.
Here in the afterlife,
forgotten, he walks
otherwise alone.
This pathway untrodden.
Looking for somewhere
to place his tomb.
Only the words spoken
seem follow him home.

The streets all the same,
only now the faces all fade.
moving people blend in
with the grey roving rain.
Endlessly pouring the spirits away.
Oblivious to the simple spectre
of what used to be true.
He floats down tear glistening streets.
Riverways to a lifetime of memories.
Memories that speak of you.

If anyone saw him,
they would shiver right through.
A mirage in the dark.
A visage of pain with no colour or spark.
A smeared glass view
that you can only just see through,
but as soon as you look,
the world becomes askew,
and recollection
starts to fade away
from you.

He walks the astral plane.
Visits old haunts,
seen through a different frame
new lenses share views of pain.
Friends downward bowed heads
crying in the downpouring rain.

Kyle Coare

To the ends of the universe and back

We can lay in the blossom.
Fields of dandelions sauntering,
roaring along with the sound
of the rushing river
and its welcoming song.
We can sit in that loving gaze
where eyes can't move in case
it's all a mistake, a mirage in the air.
To even blink could see
the image fade and slowly disappear.

We can sit and breathe
the day into yesterday, listening
for night to start twinkling
its magic light our way.
We can lay beneath glistening waterfalls.
The spray teasing us to look its way,
the majestic blue of the glowing water
tempting us to let eyes stray,
but my eyes are all over you,
drinking in every heartbeat
as if it has never tasted
anything as delicious as your memories.
The low rumbling, grumble of coursing
liquid calls, but I'd be unable to answer,
too entranced to chance a glance away,
to ever miss a moment of this day.

We can feel the soft ground beneath.
The heat from our fiery embrace
radiating into the soil as we breathe.
The air of loves beauty bequeathed.
I never want to leave, so perfect a scene,
but then, with you, any view
would be a dream,
I'd travel to the ends
of the universe and back
on your wonderous light beams.
Sitting with you and your magic gleam.

We can build a home
from the buttercups and roses,
let the irises encircled us,
protecting from
the harshest winds unkind forces.
A neon soul riding my shadow,
we can levitate to the stars.
Hearts penetrating the clouds
so that the rains wash down.
Trees serving to guide the rains
to fill the river to bathe,
to wash away the dirt of the city grime.

And every night
under our blanket
of leaves,
we can climb,
to watch the moon
and her
mysterious shine,
and listen to
the stories she weaves.

Shimmering veils

There's a place, deep in the late hours
when the clock slows down, ready to sleep.
Hands tired from slowly creeping
across the minutes on perpetual repeat.
You can feel the ripples sometimes,
when the dimming veil of twilight
and the shimmering
fantastical countryside slowly collide.

Fluid thoughts
seemingly come
from nowhere at all,
and land in your head
in a startling fall.
Evaporating into clouds
around the room,
droplets of the finest mist.
You breathe it deeply in,
like your lungs
have been left bereft of oxygen.
Your emotions start to lift,
the walls start to shift and you see
all the intricate melodies
swiftly tickling the air.

Feelings are heightened,
the darkness inviting,
shades no longer frightening.
Thoughts and memories
start fighting
to get to the forefront
of your mind,
illuminating the imagination
like a fiery bolt
of lightning.

And then it floods
like a torrential downpour,
but the rain is warm,
keeping your mind pure,
taking your flaws
and washing them away.
It is all consuming,
but not tiring.
It is soothing,
smoothing over the cracks left
so many times before,
so that you can sit
and let your thoughts
become a doorway
into a world of lore.

Upon the banks of a river called love

Let us stroll
along the banks
of this river
called love. Hope we fall in.
Feel the cool spray over your face,
as in slow motion,
you start to embrace the gentle waves.
Let the water pour over skin,
seeping through our clothing,
clinging to our bodies, a hug
warming the heart within.

Let's not dip our toes,
just drop our guards
expose ourselves
to the potential cold
and the undercurrent below.
Feel the pull of the deep depths
as little fish nibble at feet
to welcome them into the undertow.

Be shown where the river goes.
An illuminating light display,
the city seen from
such an obscure view,
as the waters cover you,
giving you a whole new
depth of view.
The river of love
will show it all to you.
It always knows
the best places to flow.

Separate our
bodies from souls,
spread out across
the waterways
like a cloud,
soaking it all in.
Now you can provide the rainfall
over deserts of deserted dreams,
I'll provide the rainbows
to share the
beauty that lies within.

And where that rainbow sits
upon the ripples at landfall,
there won't be a pot of gold,
but a locket of joy. Sharing
an image of you
and an image of me.
Staring lovingly
at each other eternally.
Which can float gently out
to the ocean of memory.

To make a call

Spectral coin
gripped, tightly in
my mitts. Sweat drips
from shaking fingertips.
So scared to lose it
or let it slip. The spray
of rain hits my face,
or are these old tear tracks
that time hasn't erased?

Coin growing hot,
glowing coin slot,
a gravitational field
pulling my fingers close.
ready to drop.

If I could
just make that call,
just a few numbers
falling from some
mystical phonebook.
A connection
to somewhere?
Nowhere?
Everywhere?
Where people
are not forgotten,
but pictures
slowly fading
into the vapours
of the air.

The digits blur
from my fingertips.
Numbers bursting
like bubbles
in the atmosphere.
Telephone line
crackles into life.
A dial tone.
A click.
A ring.
Then the magic sound
of answering.

Hello....

I can speak on a busy stage,
but how do you get those words
to conquer the universe's greatest hills?
How do those words extend
across the ever-expanding
chasm of time? A gap in reality
with no beginning or end.

Oh, to hear that voice again.
To be able to converse like time
hadn't crashed to an end.
To be able to laugh.
To start to comprehend
that this journey
isn't an ending but a chapter
somewhere near the beginning.

Impossible hearts beat in sync

We are
impossible hearts,
beating in time,
but ever so far apart.
Feeling each
rippling nerve twinge,
like waves
spreading across a vast pond.
Droplets of spray
soaring into the airways,
the cosmos,
the heavens above,
where they stay.
Forming tight bonds,
wavy liquid stars,
the very drops of our love,
lighting the heavens above
with twinkling sparks.

If I was born in
another storyline,
or I had turned left
a few times
instead of following
the right-hand line,
if you had shifted seats,
caught that train instead
of walking on blistered feet,
Would these hearts still
be holding hands?
Would they be embracing
in Disney inspired treasure islands,
and not these cities of dread?

You comfort my soul
when it's screaming inside.
You make me feel whole
when I'm only a quarter full,
because my river of hope has dried.
I feel your pull
every day and night,
like gravity showing me
loves true calling,
a majestic sight,
a magical light
beckoning me in.

I see you under
starshine awnings,
but to get there I fight to
cross a world
that's crumbling,
a sky that's falling,
an ocean yawning,
before I can get to your side,
and let your dawn
of love rise beside.

Paracusia

First you just hear silence,
your heartbeat joins in.
Soon a light blowing wind
morphs into a gale. No wait,
its swirling again. Hail.
A chanting chorus. Voices.
Noises. Telling you to fail.

This is what it feels like...

Laying alone at night. Pindrop skin.
A sound that is not there. Reality thins.
Part of a mental condition,
that is really not so rare,
but we keep quiet about it.
Misunderstandings bring fear.
They think we may be violent.
Make us keep silent,
when the sounds are oh so near.

A knock on the door.
Thud. Thud. Thud.
Three for luck
but wait,
there is no one there,
is it the winds roar?
No figure lurking, no person,
no shadows nor creatures.
Just an empty street,
so, to your seat, you return
Thud. Thud. Thud.
Again, you are stood. Alone
cold night flooding in.
Nothing again and again.
Repeat to fade. Ad nauseum.

The other noises, emboldened,
begin to join in, not wanting
to miss out on the party within.
The conversation begins.
Chatter, voices. A roomful of ghosts
and my God they love a natter.
It doesn't matter
that you are lying in bed,
or sitting watching tv instead.
Before long it's like a busy pub,
but somewhere along the way,
you have clearly upset the voices
and now they turn on you.

These sounds can't be in your head.
How can they be? *It can't be me.*
I'm hearing them swirling all around,
like a whirlpool around a dinghy at sea.

That sound, like light, a glare,
blurted images that are not there.
A flare. Swinging your way, taunting.
Haunting movements. Pounding.
Swaying across your audio vision.
Then the sounds get closer.
A fist. Connects fast.
A rumble as the jawline crumbles
and your whole world cracks,
splitting like an egg.
You hear the splash of every drop,
hitting the canvas in a belly flop
and you open your eyes again.

Alone in your room
as you have always been.

Kyle Coare

Wormholes into my dreams

Through every teardrop
of this endless rain,
I see a million worlds.
Cascading, warped
portals to other realms,
like pierced veins
to other bloodstreams.
Wormholes into my dreams.
Puddles of fantasy
to sail across in paper boats,
covered in handwritten notes
from that special heart,
the one over which my thoughts dote.

Through every twist of my head,
I see shimmering worlds.
Entrancing in their dazzled glances.
So distant, but so closely connected.
Dimensions held within ourselves.
Only disconnecting when our
pathways change.

When I shift my eyes
I see a million colours rise
through the grey surrounds,
like a vibrant dance
to long silent ethereal sounds,
mystically mixed
with the colours they inspire.
Given permission
to finally express
the love
that internally bounds
like a raging fire.

My gaze devours
every morsel
of the spectrum.
The brilliant light;
a myriad flavours,
all tasting unique
in sweetness and bite.
I long to taste the night,
but the sunlight hours
rule for now.

Through every teardrop
of this endless rain,
and the innumerable worlds
contained within.
There is one constant.
A face that smiles my way,
who lives in my dreams,
in the edges of every single fantasy.
That beauty. She speaks to me
in every single teardrop I set free.

Kyle Coare

The quiver in our chests

My frail heart quivers
as its strings
are pulled taught.
A bow ringing
the bells around
my mind so fraught.
I once sought
whispers of love,
along valleys of monsters.
Now I listen
to the hearts of others,
not those demons caught
in the darkness amongst us.

My bow-stringed
heart sings a song
to the stars.
Return the fire that you stole
to fire those pinpricks of light.
I used to be content
with the darkness.
The ink fathomless,
just me and my
ghostly travellers,
traversing
the stark blackness
that always seemed to find us.

But now instead,
I seek mysteries,
in seabed dreams.
Coral clothed depths
seed my imagination.
Until it is at critical mass,
a biomass of inspiration,
sailing through
the minds of poetic
wanderers,
searching for
pages to lay down
their dreams.

In synchronicity
we wandered
two separate cities.
Both looking for wonders
in the stone features,
both wanting something
to answer this
overpowering need.
The ever-knocking sound
of the floor pounding
a rhythm into our feet.

A heartbeat
to feed
that growing
knock
on the door,
the quiver
in our chests
always
yearning
for more.

Angel wings

Angels should never
have their silver wings clipped.
Sparkling feathers
should stay unpruned.
They should never fear
the rusty scissors sent to shear.
I'll be here to
hold you close my dear,
to administer
a daily dose of love
to help those wings
soar high above.

Just lay back.

Let the pleasure
waves take you,
all those
sores and aches
held dreamily
by the sea.
The flood of love
flowing all
over you
as you prepare
to embark upon
your journey,
your first flight
flying free.

Angels should
never fear darkness,
because the glare
of light from those
dazzling wings
shouldn't ever be dulled.
But if anyone pulls
a single feather from you,
I'll be here to repair
and aid your recovery.

So just lay back.

Let the blinding light
do its work,
showing you
islands in the sea,
snow topped mountain peaks,
the capsizing waves
crystallised
become particles in the flowing breeze.
Clouds. The most glorious sounds
and all the love that abides
here in this heart of mine.

Irises rise in beauty to the skies

I see flowers in your eyes,
irises that rise heavenly
to the skies, looking
in wonder and surprise.
Lost in a dream
of forever yesterdays
and so many
tomorrow fantasies.
Those seas you wish
to be swimming,
but no swimming gear
did you bring.
Just a costume of fear,
and some bling
of insecurity.

You see all the lies,
told to you over so many years,
personalised hate smears,
that you wear
over the face you now fear.
I see flowers in your eyes.
The beauty that you
were told wasn't true.
All the pieces of you
they viewed
and sought
to use to belittle you.
This was just them
looking through
a mirror world,
and seeing
their own reflection
painted loud and true.

I see those fears
still blossoming,
rose petal red.
Cheeks glaring
when you feel the heat
of embarrassment start
to tingle under the skin
you so wish to shred,
like a bubbling furnace
sits somewhere deep within.
You wish you were
beautiful instead.

But I also see
the strength to stand,
with your heart in hand,
letting your words spill
with the tears
that overfill your eyes,
dropping
onto the dirt and soil.
I see flowers of hurt and toil
where those tears do fall.
I see sunlight in your eyes.
I see so much beauty it shines,
and everywhere you walk
a trail of flowers
follows behind.

Murmurs across universal tides

Echoes.
Shadow words
following on from long
after the words have gone.
Letters that still float
on the slipstream
that previous words leave.

I love you.

These words
still haunt the otherwhere.
Spoken when things were clear,
before the storm shattered
the glassy air.
Gaseous word vapour
from yesteryear.

Words we should
have kept chained,
tightly tied,
gripped around our hearts.
in a locket.
The boat was sailing well
We shouldn't have rocked it.
we shouldn't have even departed
that shoreside tide.

Echoes.
Shadow words.
Let those words slip.
Don't let them rip a hole
in your already worn heart.
Don't let regret or fear
stop your stride.
Find your step,
and dance with pride.

Those echoed words
would be around,
even if you had kept them
under lock and key.
They would still sit
deeply within,
only inside,
they would have
screamed and cried.
Now instead they have
the whole universe
in which to reside.

18 hours in A&E

18 hour waiting times.
Zombies spraying hateful bile
over the rank and file,
in this overcrowded
illness fermentation tank.

"I blame those
from outside this square mile"
Coughed and splurged through alcohol fuelled
spew inducing rage, they repeatedly preach,
"It's the foreigners"
Bleating the same Daily Mail front page,
increasingly ignorant of their sheepish white faces,
swelling up with cuts and bruises.
Another night of broken fists and bloodied boozers.

Police officers chained to criminal clientele.
"But it's the foreigners"
they yell.
Repeating the call
All the way throughout nightfall,
At the Wetherspoons
NHS after party free for all.

"But it's the foreigners"
They say, wobbling
as their drunken feet sway towards
the smoking area ashtray.
They pound around waiting,
berating everyone and everything,
though their injuries are no one else's fault
but they won't admit to their own failings.

"It's all the foreigners I swear"
Blearily stumbling around,
yelling at everyone
like they are wearing a crown.
Missing their name when called.
Too plastered to hear
through their own noise.
This Wetherspoons tribe
letting anyone with ears
listen to their vomit and diarrhoea
swilled diatribe.

Filled with curses and swears,
all in the name of shifting blame.
*"Those ne'er do wells have
caused this waiting game."*
They frame their arguments with fits
of pounding fists, this wild bunch of angry
spoiled hypocrites,
as they continue to stagger, spew and swear.
"Not my fault officer I swear"
"Stop the boats" I hear,
in between background cries,
"Fix the system, it is broken" they wail.
Well, let me give you a surprise
in the form of a rhymed tale.

You all voted for this.
Brexit Britain IS falling to bits,
because of the leaders and all of you hypocrites,
who don't want foreigners on our shores.
Those that wish to see our services pawned.
The very same people you blame
Are the ones keeping our boat afloat.
Throw them to the waves and you too will capsize.
I'd say look with your own eyes,
but they seem so clouded with hate and bad tides.

Kyle Coare

Moonlit candelabra

Dull feint light,
mysterious twilight,
like a moonlit candelabra
dusting the day with delight.
Masking the day
with shades of night.
In this space I can stretch out,
let my fraught mind race,
running through thoughts
until some inspiration falls
upon my pages

I've always liked
drinking down the darkness,
feeling it trickle slowly, warmly
down my throat.
Each tingle sends a spark, a sprinkle,
jolting my heart,
pulsing to my brain.
Raining down notes
to turn into word refrains.

I love the way the inky deep blue residue
of night-time consumes you,
seeps over you, worming through
your internal wiring. Every vein, artery,
every nerve ending firing,
before ending at your fingertips
and oozing back out again,
raining through the pores
in an outflowing of pure unfiltered imagination,
like spring water from the earths veins.
You smother your hands in this artistic fluidity
and splash it across your page.

I've always loved the nighttime,
the calm,
the rustle of leaves
like delicate windchimes,
but the darkness sometimes
lets others in.
Shadows creeping,
dispiriting the sublime,
like your frayed nerves,
stretched taught and thin,
unearthly vines, spindly and withering.
They suck the imagination like straws under skin,
gulping down every feeling deep within,
leaving your mind weak, wobbling, reeling.
Reaching for just a piece of a silver lining.

But fear not
these beasts
cannot stay upon this
dimensional pathway,
the energy of night
makes them shiver and sway,
before the imagination they sunk,
becomes fear in their veins.
and soon the moonlight
will hold you tight again,
letting your imagination,
once again play.

In the darkness of my mind's eye

I lay in the dark
thinking of you
and I start to
tear away
the night-time sky,
feeling fragments of midnight
become reality in my grasp.
I pull the dreams apart,
bringing
the pieces
a little closer
to me,
closer
to my heart.

Worn strands of the sky
sing a gasped song,
stars stand alight
with stories I'd die to know.
Mysteries held
in the marvels of space,
I'd long to see their
galactic monuments,
their mystical glow
etched in the celestial memory trace.

In the darkness
of my mind's eye
I start to see light.
Cosmic paintings
of your perpetually
beautiful face.
Carved eternally
to this eyelid resting place.

I let my thoughts fall
to all the aborted tomorrows,
the future pathways
destroyed in the blink of an eye.
I sigh
at how
one waved
goodbye
can see so many
futures die.
I think of those universes,
ending
before they ever
truly got to begin.
Ending
through fear,
fear of letting a feeling
tease the omnipresent skin
of a universe that already knows
what I'm thinking.

In the darkness
of my mind's eye.
I see flames rising high.
Inside I want to cry,
at my own pride,
the fear of being
left alone striding along
the roadside.
When that is where
I roam alone every
uneventful eventide,
instead of just saying
a brisk hello
and sharing a kiss
with the happy sky.

Cognitive purgatory

I'm whining
across this other side
that I'm seemingly
confined within.
A cognitive purgatory.
A mental penitentiary.
This place, a prison cell.
Chaining up my
wayward thoughts
so they can no longer fly free.

There is writing
lining the walls, but those
words are hidden from me.
Too frightening for me to see?
My eyes are hiding the story.
I'm pining after a dream,
yet sleep is evading me.
I feel her someplace close, but
her face is somewhere I can't see.

I'm feeling ill tonight.
Not physically unwell
but mentally, going through hell,
like a murder of crows
has decided to roost
inside my mind.
They keep pecking
at my thoughts,
digging up long
worn-out threads,
then dropping them
in my mental lap.
Wriggling worms of the head.
Now, there is no way I can nap.

I want a psychic cuddle,
as a real one is unlikely
to come knocking,
and honestly
if it does,
I will be more
than just a little confused.
A disembodied
pair of arms,
wrapping around me,
like some weird face-hugger
from an alien movie.
That may just scare
the living daylights
out of me.

I need to dream,
but my eyes
are pinned wide open
like two gaping mouths
mid scream.
I want to dream,
to see the face I see,
to be in that place
where beauty breathes,
because I'm feeling
seriously lost in this
so-called reality.

If I flew

If I flew
the same way that
time soars past,
I'd be moving too fast.
I'd miss the
exquisite scenery
as it blurs away below me.
I'd miss all the telling
glances directing me to look
into their eyes
at the magic you can see,
and as time advances
I'd be lost and alone.
My heart would slowly
turn to stone,
ice crystals enclosing it,
steadily fusing with the bone.

If I grew
like my heart
beats for you,
a rhythm that builds majestically,
I'd soon be a planet entity,
complete with a bunch of moons,
but then people would
walk all over me,
take advantage
of my atmosphere, fill my air,
with choking exhaust fumes.
Would there be any space left for me
and would any of them care?

If I wrote
all of my feelings
then set them alight
to join with the
twinkling stars in the sky,
then I'd ignite the stratosphere.
The night would be like day,
but all the beautiful stars
would hide away,
I'd stand in the ash filled grey,
alone,
without a soul to show the way.

If I took a moment,
would I hold on to it forever,
never put it back,
keep it securely
in my trusty backpack,
with all my scraps of paper,
the unwritten love letters,
and the ones written
but never sent.
The whatevers, the whenevers,
the lousy shreds of unbound papers,
that I keep in torn tethers,
like a paper jigsaw to remind
of where I've been.
Some passages would be underlined,
to mine for gold in the secrets within.
Would I take that moment
and share it with you?
So that we can forever cherish
this world and explore
all of the places with eyes renewed.

Seedling

Deprived of oxygen,
sallow skin,
guts sinking
into the dirt below.
Mind struggling,
thoughts not linking.
Everything is running slow.
Internal computer lights
are blinking,
the cursor circle
is constantly spinning.
Memory banks
no longer thinking.
Ages since I've felt this low.

Just a lone seedling trying
to break through this earth
and grow, but all I feel is dirt
and darkness, crushing my chest,
so that the air in my lungs won't flow.
Oxygen not in abundance.
There doesn't seem to be
any sustaining substance.
I'm just stuck here
somewhere deep
in the ground below.

I see a glimmer
of light in you,
life beams out
from your internal glow.
I see a sight
I want to view.
The beauty
of a summer sun,
surrounded
by flowers
all breaking
through.

So, I will find
a way to grow,
build myself big,
strong and true.
So I can share
all of my dreams with you.

Kyle Coare

A lungful of silent screams

I am the silent screams
that fall from
pain-numbed lips.
Full of words
that burn to be heard,
but so scared
that my words
will turn to a blaze,
igniting me
and those I love
in the flames.
I fear what may slip,
if the sizzling embers start to spit.
Eviscerating the hope
I try to hold within.

I'm trapped here.
Just me and these welled up tears,
which threatened to burst
like a dam smashing out of me.
I see other people,
but they are like ghosts.
Smeared around the edges,
homeward they float.

I'm surveying the blue privacy screens,
the monitor beeping, the machine
with numbers that mean nothing to me,
except that things inside
are not quite how they should be.
I'm seeing glimpses of faces,
just as distant and as lost as I feel.
Sweat peels down my face,
my fearful pulse races,
my heart keeps giving chase.

Vampires sucking blood
at every chance they can get,
pinprick arms, inkblot skin.
Lone hours wept trying to stop
worries from creeping in.
In wards of inwardly
aimed self-neglect,
I just let time pass.

My signal falls,
no mayday to call,
no one hears me gurgle
through the wash of liquidity
clogging my lung walls.

I call again.
Gasped nothings swirl out.
Nothing will connect.
I'm just here waiting for the reaper
to come,
my soul to collect.

Can I survive this night?
I'm full of doubt
and a bucketful of fright.

I'm waiting for anything at all.
A moment of clarity befalls.
Breathlessly gasping,
mind climbing the walls
but I know deep within
that each passing moment,
every fleeting beat
of my reaching heart,
puts me a little closer
to where better feelings start.

Under fibreglass skies

At night,
the shadows stalk.
Whispers heard
in reversed talk.
Haggard shapes walk by,
drip stands held tight.
Mysterious masses
hover nearby,
hunching over
like shepherds' watching
their flock under a red sky.

Under fibreglass skies,
ceiling tiles pockmarked
with smoke detection devices,
acne scars over feint light.
Flightless I lay,
unable to make
sense of the change
from night to the day.

Gentle beeping,
the rhythmic breathing
of oxygen machines wheezing.
The sleepy feeling
slowly enveloping me,
I sink into my own eyes,
into the darkness
that sits behind.

Peaceful
slumber drifts
like detritus
on the inky depths
of darkness.
The soft exhales
of midnight sounds,
ruffle the sails,
taking us to
peaceful paradise.
Toning the
nightmares down
for just one
more night.

Kyle Coare

A taste of heaven

I want to feel your skin,
naked, to feel every breath,
the curved roads
that life has shaped.
Teasing my fingers
down your country lanes,
sharing paradise
as hot blood pulses
through our veins,
I want to see your eyes,
excited by the new sunrise.

A road map of your life.
Wherever you've walked,
I'd follow the trail left.
I'd swim in the lakes you dived.
I'd take slow breaths,
to prolong every second.
So, I can hold them
tightly for eternity.

I want to bask
in your glow.
Feeling the
sustaining light
that you throw
like a second sun to those
that see your beauty.
The outer and inner
light show,
a tantalising taste
of heaven,
and what is
forever to follow.

I want to walk
in your footsteps.
Never to push ahead,
nor to overreach or overstep.
I want your stars to shine
like a sky full of diamonds
glistening over a lakeside retreat.
I will listen to your fears,
I'll give all of me to help you
find that internal light
when darkness nears.

I want your mind
to shower me
in its amazing power,
let its magic
tower over
everything.
We can sit
at the top
and listen
to the universe sing.
I'd glance
into those eyes
and find forever
sitting waiting
within.
A taste of heaven
still fragrant on my lips
from that timeless special moment,
that very first shared kiss.

The constant stream

They come and go.
A river of faces,
a liquid flow,
the colourful
waterway races,
whilst below
this weeping tree,
I sit,
a still mournful
shadow.

The ebbs and flows
as the water
slowly rises
to rageful
stormy tides,
then subsides.
My mind takes
long boat rides,
feeling the rhythm
awaken the insides.

Beside the banks,
I sit in internal conversation,
watching the frothing waves.
Sleepily shaving away
minutes of the day.
Gentle aromas
of pastry and coffee
briefly help me see
my surroundings more clearly,
before the steam and condensation
fogs my glasses obscuring
the constant stream
ever so slightly.

Coffee shop window seat,
complete with flowers
to deceive the winter
into believing it had emerged
too soon.
Caressing a warming cup of tea.
Wrapped snuggly, lovingly
in this
bubble cocoon,
I feel strength
beginning to rise
from my stinging toes,
taking detours
through my body
to repair
my aching
worn-down bones.
Letting it revive me
from my frail
stumbling stride,
inspiring the art
that beats inside.

Outside the window,
the ever-flowing tide.
Not stopping, not breathing,
just forcing their lungs
to help keep their feet
marching
to their beats
in time.

Kyle Coare

Overhead light

Overhead light
never goes out.
Across the eerie clockface
the expanding hours
quake slowly by.
A slow shadow looms.
Ticking hands of doom,
show minutes consumed,
never hours.
Merely witness
to momentous
monotonous
moments, entombed,
deep in
the midnight gloom.

Nightmares swirl in
during the low
hours of doubt,
like sand blowing
across the desert of time.
Alien bursts from
stomach-ache wounds.
To take over the ward,
anxious shouts heard
from terrified lungs.
Fear explodes,
clouded by worry
sung so loud.
A beeping flurry
alarming dawn chorus.
As the sounds
of morphine nights
fade merrily away from us.

I hear traffic
passing by
in grinding
agony outside.
Then silence.
The outside
devoured in a bite,
and it's all bringing
me down.
The sounds
ringing around,
the visions stalking
the ground,
footsteps that pound,
prowling the corridors
so loud,
but no one appears.
No figure peers,
just an invisible
witness to my tears?
Or a ghost,
who has been
stuck here for years?
Merely visiting?
Or here to stay?

Only lone atoms in a vast universe

I awaken
at a godforsaken
hour. My brain aching,
from all the avalanching words
shaking, trying to evade the
branching stories reach,
attempting to shower out
all over me.

It's no use,
I can't stop turning
the empty pages.
A deluge rain
falls suddenly.
Hopefully it will cease
my sullen brain
from burning.

This island cursed
with the worn-out
remnants of torn
word cloud bursts.
Not yet ready to be traversed,
these thoughts have been submerged,
in the dark for days,
kept, trapped, held back, kidnapped,
backed up, blocking my airways.

Now unearthed.
they regurgitate,
trying to vomit out,
wanting to erupt,
a rainbow
of thoughts,
worries and doubts,
to become immersed
in a bright new world
of words and verse.

Even though
sleep is needed,
I need to write
these seedlings down
before they fade into dust.
A cluster bomb blast of words
bursts across your mind,
these thoughts unravel,
spraying out like heavy shrapnel,
or dropping like a cartoon anvil.
You have to scrabble around
to catch the pieces
as they float sky bound,
before they disperse
into the atmosphere,
making the images disappear
somewhere out of your reach,
becoming only lone atoms
in a vast universe.

On these bittersweet days

You may
not be here in body,
but you live in every pore.
Every story that soars
through our thoughts.
You still sit in your old seat,
slightly worn, still moulded
to your shape, your presence.
Your form is in the fabric
of this reality.
The settee facing the tele.
Your sanctuary.

You may not be here in body,
but you were always here in soul.
The soundtrack of my childhood.
Marvin Gaye spitting truth.
What's going on? You would say.
You'd be questioning everything.
When we look to space for guidance,
your answers still dance through our ears.
Your mind, the streetlights
on darkened beckoning pathways,
and on these bittersweet days
I let the joy you brought
flow in like sun rays,
to part the chill darkness of hurt
and illuminate the way.

You may not be here in body,
but I still see you every day.
In everything we do,
I see reflections of you.
All you taught us.
All the good that lived within you
still sits in that worn out seat,
and in the air we breathe,
in every particle of air,
in every stray feather
we see lying there.
You never truly leave.
Not with all the stories
you bequeath.

Kyle Coare

Become the waters

I dreamt a dream,
I slept on moonbeams, sleeping soundly
for the first time in forever.
You came to me like a rose petal
blowing on the breeze.
I handed myself to you on a plate,
and said,

"Take whatever you need
My voice, my words, all that I am.
I grant it freely. Use it wisely."

I want you to sail over my endless seas,
I've become the waters,
one with this seascape memory.
I want you to find
all of the treasure I've buried for you,
every glisten of gold, the ancient texts I hold
the secrets untold in stories,
I'll hand you all of my truth.

In dreams,
words were imparted
like the parting seas,
showing us new pathways
through our mysteries.
Whole landscapes shifted,
splintered into fragments anew.
We could see the truth.
Hear it on the wind,
the words that sang
of love, the gift that never ends.

They showed us forever,
and all that's ever been,
as we floated like feathers
through this formerly
underwater scene.
Across shipwrecks
lost to times
discarded logbooks.
We chanced to look,
and the scene was divine,
a colossal ravine
with colours dancing
across our eyes
to the hidden song
of time.

"Let's stay
and see all the sights
these fluid eyes can see"

The magic that floats like a cloud
beneath the rippling surface.
Set it all free and reinvent
every twirling vortex of this
broken history,
to mould into our own
miraculous story.
Yours and mine.

Then I realise,
we can visit these places
anytime we close our eyes,
and the true magic lives
in the embrace
of you and I.

Slow motion

Becoming very well acquainted
with the backs of my eyelids
in this drowsy weekend world
of hospital slow motion fluidity.
You can close your eyes
and see the totality.
All of time, painted in
tonally shifting colours that
seep all over you.

If you glance even further
into the middle distance,
you may chance to catch eyes
with the wonderous woman
of the skies, who sifts through
these places from time to time.

Slip between veils,
deep blue privacy blinds
between the dream worlds
and real life,
It's so hard to know
what is solid state
and what exists only in that
perplexing place which lines the mind,
it all blends into one in a stunning display
of peaceful sublimity.
Leaving you dancing along the
shimmering timeline,
and deep into the arms of infinity.

The endlessly
marching beat,
beds empty then fill,
seats taken,
become empty,
in the blink of an eye,
time slips
across the clock,
it doesn't recognise
the way the day lies.

A new face blurs
into the scene,
momentarily there
before a hazy shade
clouds the air
and they wisp away.
Just a dream
drifting into
the images that spill
across the veil
of the real and unreal.

Kyle Coare

A storm within a hurricane

Our skin breathing as one.
A storm
within
a hurricane.
A whirlwind
in a tornado.
We swirl together
like cream
through our perfectly
blended dreams,
wishing to taste
the extraordinary.
Those special moments
where our shallow breaths
become hollowed out screams.

Fear disintegrated,
disinterested
in trying to trip us,
nor trying to trick us,
just treat us
to those moments
where shared heartbeats
are our symphony
and the choir of birds
are singing along.

Left to
ourselves,
naked as the day
we were born.
The sounds
of the world meld
into one.
Only our touches matter,
now the fear in
ourselves has gone.
We devour every inch,
every morsel of flesh.
Hunger insatiable,
I need you more
than I need another breath,
anything else feels
like a slow death.

Two souls entwined,
became one combined.
Two parts of one united sign.
Even when the skies start to bend,
and the lights start to blind.
Those souls are like
two shooting stars
forever aligned.

Kyle Coare

Brick dust futures

Through tear smeared vision
I see a window, sharing
brick dust futures.
A cracked wall, crumbling,
but not yet ready to fall.
I don't know what lies
beyond it all,
it could just be
a brickwork facade, a fantasy,
but it offers me hope
of a life, a little more ordinary.

I see red brick
facing back at me,
cementing itself
until it becomes
a concrete memory.
It could be
someplace else entirely,
I'm picturing a riverside getaway.
Anything that can replace
this aching void I contemplate,
this empty space,
with wretched faces
coming and going,
too-ing and fro-ing.
I'd much rather a waterway
where the future is flowing.

This red wall has me intrigued,
my fatigued mind
starts to imagine daydreams,
a lush field of green
where I can lay,
undisturbed,
mind unperturbed
by the daily grind. I can lay
beneath the sunbeams all day,
soaking up their energy,
breathing the cleansing air deep.
Just sat watching
the willow weep,
as I slowly, peacefully
relax into sleep.

The view could be
a bit more enticing,
showing me something
all together more exciting,
but it's more about
what lies out of view.
Beyond that wall
is a world that feels new.
It could be a fairytale
straight from the page,
or a dream released
from the cage in my brain,
but whatever sits
beyond that pale red brick,
is a whole new life
that I've not yet lived.

A felled oak

Like a felled oak
I lay on that forest floor,
surrounded by the debris
of the person I was before.
I wish away
a dream of bliss,
I kiss away a breath
from these aging lips.
I sit awaiting death.
Just a felled oak
with nothing left.

An insect lands inspecting
my stretched-out limbs,
my hands pulling
the sky blinds down,
to block the rush
of reality pouring in.
That insect is joined, gradually
by sanctuary seeking
songbirds flocking
from the threatening
thunder clouds above.
I wish away hope
but realise I can never
wish away love.

The sky splits,
Thors hammer hits.
Blam.
Night is day
and back again.
A magical sound
like wind chimes
playing a rousing refrain.
The rain falling
between the leaves.
The surrounding trees
keeping me covered
from the worst
of this ripped
open sky vein.

And the surge comes in,
not rainwater rushing,
but the forests neighbours
seeking refuge. Our friends,
feathered, furry or scaled,
small or big, they all came,
and into
my open arms
they hid
from the worst
of the storm.

Catch a passing raindrop heart

If you took out
my beating heart
and planted it
deep in the earth,
like a crimson beating seed.
Would it feed from nature?
Would it grow
into a big bold flower?
Petals ever thirsty,
always open to catch
any stray droplets
of love within.

Could the love inside
catch a passing
raindrop heart?
Or would it fall
like rainbow drops?
Forming a teardrop puddle,
a shallow pool
in this forest hollow,
where the bark
sits broken apart
by storms
that once followed sunshine,
now can only wallow
watching the skyline.
Hoping for brighter
lights to follow.

Could this heart, so wide,
open up like a vast countryside?
To give the tears from above
a home they can adore and love.
As they form rivers
over this pulsing crust,
could they sidetrack the misery?
Avoiding the grey concrete floor
of this fading city.
Only here for the scenery,
the flora and fauna
that plays so heavenly.

Could this hollow heart
take every droplet of love,
this pulsing goblet, encrusted with
the finest crimson gems.
The perfect vessel
to store it all safely within.
Could it flood these streets
when times are grim?

Could this straining heart
stop any love from draining away?
Would it seep through the cracks?
Or would it stay?
Ready for the day
it is filtered through
the petals, like a watering can
letting the love flow
through every single one of us,
cleansing this world of grime and dust,
nourishing the hurt
until it blooms into a flower
that towers over all of us.

Kyle Coare

Kiss of life

Stop this chill that envelops
my heart. A blanket of darkness
clogging my arteries,
until it needs a restart.
I feel no breath within my lungs,
when our song isn't being sung.
So, hold me tight.
I want to feel the still warmth
against the frost of night.
Press yourself into my skin tonight.
I'll try not to hide.
I'll peel away my layers
so you can see inside.

Let us feel every rise
and fall of life,
every breath, let us sway
upon its vibrations,
like a shooting star
cutting across
grand constellations.

I'll mould like putty around you,
hold you until forever
says goodnight,
and eternity welcomes us
over the threshold into her insight.
I'll turn out the light.
Just to heighten our senses.
I want to feel our defences fall.
Kiss me and I'll howl like the wolf.
Hungry, listening to the moons
silent call.

Kiss me quick.
I need the kiss of life
placed upon my lips.
As I take a sip
let me slip into fantasy,
just to hear you
whisper to me,
those words
that taste like honey.
Those three little words,
that stand tall
like giants of vocabulary.
We can welcome the butterflies
the roses and the trees.
Let us become one
with nature under that
ceiling of leaves.

Let's feel hot breath
blowing away
the lingering
slow death.
Instead let us hold
tightly to the bed,
and let forever
share with us
her stories.
As we whisper
sweet nothings,
that could
awaken the dead.

The dreamer

The dreamer lies,
eyes heavy, hungry
to see what sits
behind the veiled night.
He longs to see your eyes,
to find that unique click in time,
where everything stops.
The flickering hands stick.
The rain of time pauses mid drop.

The dreamer flies
over uncharted seas
towards undiscovered islands
of mystery,
worlds we don't usually see.
Not with our eyes
so distorted and polluted
by the world we perceive.
All in search of that glance
that spans the entirely
of existence,
to find the place it began.
Where the clock that never expires,
became one with the
hands flowing across these skies,
on timeless birds of flight.

The dreamer sighs,
eyes looking,
searching for signs
in the inky blackness that lines
the twisting rooms of his mind.
The rooms where waterfalls rushed
to smash to dust the walls.
Damming his pathway forward.
Leaving his life crushed,
under debris that flowed down
the cobwebbed halls
and the ticking sound
that grew louder and louder.

The dreamer cries,
happy tears mingle
with the sad remnants
of years gone by, to form a river
for his raft. His lifeboat to keep afloat
on his journey to find answers
to the questions
he can't find the words to emote.
And on this boat
he can float to distant shores,
where he can merge
his story with yours.
To create a new future history,
to slow the creaking
hands of time to a crawl.

Kyle Coare

Unfolded road map

Pull apart my chest
and take away
this wounded heart,
unfold it like road map.
Hold on tight
as we take
this bumpy path.
The scars show
where hidden treasures
have amassed.
We just need to watch
the countryside pass.

Pull out the stops,
twist the gear on the music box,
let the sounds in, my dear.
Every service station between
here and that final destination
is another step nearer
to the place where
the air is clear.

Tear out my eyes,
everything I've witnessed,
feed it all back to me
in word pictures,
use them to describe
the world like a dream.
That magic way
a child's painting
portrays the day.
I want to picture the sunbeams
with a face that gleams,
not the dark stain that clouds
the visions I've seen.

Take away my nose,
that pleasantly powerful
perfume now flows
through my lungs,
like the cleanest freshest oxygen.
It knows that to keep me going on
I need to breathe deep,
so that it accents my brain
with the floral scent
of an herbal tea
that has been finely steeped.
Just hold on to me
as we take a descent,
riding the low road
until we can rise again.

Take my ears, your voice now
circulates my head.
In the late hours
when I'm pondering the world,
but I should be asleep in bed,
It's your voice that sews me in
to my night-time fantasy story.
It's your voice
that contains the answers
to untold mysteries.
It's your voice
that is the needle to my thread,
stitching me into the velvet sky
amongst the clouds above,
so very high.
It's your voice
that gives me the answers
to that long held question…

Why?

Wherever this current chooses to flow

I ride the highs
and dive with the lows,
wherever this current
chooses to flow.
I let the water take my hand,
leading me to its promised land.

I fly further upstream,
as thermals lift me.
Up in the clouds,
watching sunbeams
dance down to the ground.
I don't control the wind,
I'm just a passenger
hitching a ride on the breeze.
My wings just catch
the breath which gently weaves
across the green glow
of the patchwork countryside
laced down below.
It takes me where I need to be.
Not necessarily where I want to go,
but it always has its own plans for me,
so, I just go along with the flow.

I shiver through the cold
and sizzle in the heat,
walking on scorching sands
or freezing concrete.
I go wherever
the guiding hands point.
My internal compass
feels the eternal pull
and it guides my feet
to make my life feel full.

I weather storms,
soaking my worn-out shoes,
splashing in the flooded residue.
Oblivious to the
water seeping through.
I flail in gale force winds,
in hail I take the hits.
pelted by jagged ice bits.
Sandblasted in sandstorm nights,
under a moon which wants to cry,
but has witnessed
too much misery in her life,
now her eyes have run dry.

I keep on going,
I have no choice,
the winds keep blowing.
They set my course.
Over the rivers,
from source to the sea.
I'll follow wherever
those waterways
are flowing,
to be who
I need to be.

Kyle Coare

Ode to my duvet

You hold me tight,
warming like
a devoted lover.
Knowing to not
overheat or smother,
but instead to provide
a perfect pair of arms
for me to dive within
so I can swim deep
in comforting dreams
as I rest my head
under your loving moonbeams.

You keep me
safe and sound.
Away from
the beings that
creep around,
pounding along
the floors at night.
No ghoul can sink
it's teeth down deep,
or scratch those vicious claws
into my weakened skin.
They can't get within
this barricade
you helped me build
to protect myself
from fright.

You keep me company,
listen to my stories,
picture my dreams
reading their stories along with me.
You try to withhold
the nightmares,
keeping those beasts
away from the doors.
Though sometimes
they crawl through the linings
of unfolded sleepy thoughts.
Causing pain
to roar like lightening
and my
blood to pour
from deep inside of me.

You hold me,
a beacon
of light like the moon on high,
or a lighthouse upon
the stormy rocks at night.
Showing safe passageway
towards the docks at high tide.
From deep in your cocoon
I hear the outside clocks,
knowing the hour will be soon
when the sun swaps shifts
with the lustrous moon,
and the morning birds flock.

Background scenery

Teenagers hang in their palace.
Big Macs and McFlurry highs,
golden arch towers. glow across eyes
like a youthful rite of passage.
We all did this. Our first escapes
from childhood to adultness,
but when did all of this
become so different?
Back then we were loud,
but we kept ourselves
to our own little crowds.
We didn't prowl around
like we were there to terrorise.
We didn't try to instil
fear into other people's lives.

We were just
background scenery,
not the main stars in
some unfinished balladry.
We were background
images painted
across the stage of life.
Not the fallen lives,
cut down by flick knives,
in some long-forgotten
Shakespearean tragedy.

All we wanted was to have fun.
Find others to share it with.
Explore the gifts, a world of
glass fronted lifts, searching
marble tiles for a stolen kiss
and a moment of bliss.
The most pain we would feel...
The shame of losing
a game of laser quest,
or the teenage heartbreak
when unrequited eyes
don't connect.

Our weapons of choice,
straws from McDonald's.
Plenty of chewed up paper.
That we fired upon each other
in moments of boredom.
Never anything heavier,
never anything that would
make blood run. Never anything
that would cause tears for anyone.

What happened to
the innocence of youth?
When did it become so lost?
Can it be found again?
When did we become
so territorial, so angry, so nasty?
Maybe it was when they
started to tell us that everyone else
was the enemy?
Was it when they started
to take our futures away?
Or was it when they closed down
our places to explore imagination and play?

Kyle Coare

Waterfall of light

In stunned silence,
the midnight clouds
conspire to form an alliance,
framing the moon,
so we night owls
can witness her fire.
Magnificence in heavenly pyres.
The stars bow in union,
a flowing waterfall of lights.
Spraying the night.
Giving their princess
the admiration she deserves,
her space in the light.

The wolf howls in appreciation
at the entertaining light-show greeting
that the exuberant sky is maintaining.
In the wolfs fleeting mind
he sees perfection, glistening,
like winter-frost coated pavements,
an open doorway
upon a world of everything.

The shy hedgehog,
shakes shivery spines,
distracted by
the wonderland
of a winter sky.
Fairies relighting
the stars,
one by one,
singing to themselves
a gentle winters song.

The lone man stands
on his doorstep,
shivering away
the creeping cold grip,
that has slowly
taken hold of his hands,
to lead him towards
sleep entrusted islands.
"Sleep can wait" he says,
watching the stars
as they gleefully play

Bones like icicles
keep his skin from
puddling into the paving stones.
He looks with eyes crusted
towards the snow crystal hearts.
The early sand-drift
of sleep dust,
making the view
swiftly part.
Leaving only
the ever-illuminating moon,
the perfect ending
to a tiring day.

Kyle Coare

Never-ending corridors

I once believed I'd floated down
these corridors for the final time.
These memory-stained lime walls
etched with my still vivid recollections,
like a ringing bell chime call.
Somewhere in the annals of history
the echoes once tolled for me.

I really thought
I had done with this place,
but alas, here is where
my feet once again pace.
A slight wobble to my step,
dizziness has crept
awkwardly across my mind,
forgetfulness has leapt in,
taking its space.
For now, I'm a little lost at sea
and I don't know what is happening to me.

The 3 prior times left me close to the edge,
teetering, wobbling,
just one breath of wind away from calamity.
One gust of air and I'd be damned you see.
One blast of weather
and I'd have been falling for eternity,
whether or not I saw the edge
coming closer to me.
But it appears I'm due another setback.
The same old soundtrack
like nails attacking a chalkboard.
Screaming down the aisles,
screaming down the corridors,
and that was all just me.

Yelling from a place
I never knew existed,
pain like a red-hot poker,
blistering my insides.
Pain untenable.
I'm losing the fight within.
My vision crowding.
Pain unimaginable
until the fingers of morphine
pick me up and place me gently
down again somewhere upon a cloud.

I see some dreams
stalking around,
but also hear nightmares
squawking aloud,
squirming through
the crawlspace in my mind
creating a place for themselves,
and burrowing inside.
In this world,
I'm surrounded by ghosts,
I believed, foolishly,
that I'd revisited them all,
reburied the bones,
but it appears I fear,
I still have a few more
terrors to re-home
and a few more tombstones
to carve
from my own
aching moans.

The soundless words of a kiss

I don't need you to sing to me,
nor sprinkle your magic wordplay across the moon,
dusting me entirely. Just look into my eyes intently,
I'll read the unspoken words in your dilated pupils.
I don't crave whispered words, spoken delicately,
like the breath of a summer tune uttered seductively
into my enclosed room, nor lovebirds singing melodically
a song to bless. I only need your sweet loving caress.

I don't desire a letter filled with the flow
of sweet handwriting, glowing with metaphors,
growing between sentences as they start to form
across the pages below. Save the trees a little agony.
I don't need sonnets or odes, proclaiming of love
on passionate roads. I just need you.
So, hold me tight, look deep into my eyes.
More words live in those glanced emotions
than atoms that bubble in stormy oceans.

I don't need essays expressing your feelings.
Those three simple words don't need speaking.
I hear them in the breath of the wind.
I just need your eyes to glance my way.
The words will sway deep in this playful
waltz of eyes, where they will pirouette
gently into my gaze, dancing a two-step,
to wave a fond farewell to the day.

Undressing the night with just the way
our glances connect, in a hug so tight.
Your words full of poetry,
fluffy clouds to share feelings,
can still never express the powerful healing
the magic of love brings. So don't try to sing.
Our hungry lips touching will confide everything.

I'm not in need of written declarations,
big celebrations or loving flirtations.
Just send me a kiss a day,
wrapped in your perfume bouquet.
I don't need your love to rush out,
in an emotionally written downpour.
Nor to get caught in a flurry
of stormy sounds. I don't need
the lightning to erupt from your word clouds
to illuminate shared feelings. I can already feel
the atoms reverberate whenever you are around.
I can already hear my heartbeat,
pounding through the walls of my chest,
just wanting to edge that little bit closer to perfect.

I'll always promise my heart, arrow embedded deep
from when cupids bow fired upon me,
the pointed arrowhead will always magnetically
seek that perfume, like a compass of love
showing me the right pathway to follow.
That waterside hollow, in amongst
the roses that weep,
where hearts take a leap above the moon,
where forever, just beyond the zooming stars
is a world of pure perfection.
where spiral hearts glow, bestowing their love
upon anyone that walks the pathway below.
Let our eyes take the chance to dive
into a trancelike lovers embrace,
deeper into the rainbow space
where lakes of a million shades flow.
Hearts race all around, fluttering like birds.
Lips tasting the future
in a kiss that says
so much more than words.

Still dreaming

Dreaming,
just dreaming…

A world no longer seeped in misery,
teeming with tears; wept for children
taken long before their years.
A world where colour doesn't bring pain,
race is embodied in the everyday,
culture embraced, not banished away.
Religion no longer used as excuse for war,
just as a tool to help us explore.
A world where the poor need not beg for more,
and shelter from the rain is available to everyone,
regardless of circumstance or income.
Where food banks are redundant,
a banquet for every table,
and love is abundant
not some fairytale or fable.

Dreaming…
I was just dreaming…

A world I want to believe in.
Where the seas are not seen as borderlines,
if someone wants to live in any land, It's fine.
Where the lines on maps are scrapped,
replaced with open signs.
Divide and rule has always been the way,
keep us at each other's throats,
so, we ignore what they do or say.
I say welcome everybody,
show that there is
always another way.

Dreaming...
I was dreaming...

Of the world we could be living,
the stories we could be reading.
When we all find hope
instead of tying a rope
around others' throats,
and claiming they are enemy.
Dreaming of a world
where the monsters
are no longer sleeping soundly
in control of everything,
Whilst we sit fearful under our beds,
too scared to raise our tearful heads.

I was dreaming...
Just dreaming...

Of a world where bad tides wash away
the injustices we see day to day.
Where money doesn't control
what we do or say.
Where those with more
don't get to exploit the poor,
to pour a little more struggle at their doors.

I was just dreaming...
Just dreaming...
Dreaming...

But now I've awoken
into another nightmare,
it looks just like any other day.

Kyle Coare

Close-proximity alarm

I wish I had
a close-proximity
alarm system on life,
like a car
reversing blind,
so, I can blend
into the shadows
when it beeps
saying people
are around.

Don't get me wrong,
human contact is fine.
In fact, at times,
it is divine,
but sometimes I'm too
crowded in my own mind,
that even another voice speaking
is like a theatre hall
all shouting down at you.

I wish I had a sensor
detecting when I'm
going to be in contact.
So that I can make sure
everything is fully vetted,
checked against my records,
making sure they
are not wanted in 5 countries
for crimes of neglect and affray

Again,
I'm not
anti-social.
I love people,
but I can only juggle
a couple before my mind
starts
to crumble.
My batteries
run on full power
burning out so fast,
that I soon
become flat,
even though
barely any time
has elapsed.

Kyle Coare

Acrylic dreams

I feel that surge rush
through me again,
like an ocean wave
pushing in,
then pulling me
out to sea.
A strong energy,
strangely enticing.
It holds me,
like a storm cloud bound
inland, across my island mind.
I hear it. Surging.
I feel it purging any hurt
from within,
urging me to seek out
the hope that's left
in my skin, softly tingling.

The sound rumbles
inside.
I feel...
Alive.
Into currents
I want to dive.
Down deep
into the sweet embrace
of those rippling waters,
mingling in between the waves.
Feeling the gentle rocking
of your fluid emotion
flowing over my skin.

I want to share with you
mountain views,
I want butterflies
to nest inside of you,
so, you will always feel the flutter
that says I'm thinking of you.
I want you to taste the atmosphere,
electricity zipping everywhere,
as we glide through the air
in our own magical display of gratitude,
to this universe that put us here.

I feel the pull of the tide,
the swell of the waters riding high.
I look to the moon,
as she sits beaming with pride.
I wish you could see it too,
through my minds distorted view.
That glow on her face. That glorious smile.
I'd show you so much,
the miles and miles
of magical scenery.
The forests and rivers,
the countryside greenery.
The hills and the valleys,
the seas and the sands,
all scrawled out
in an acrylic dream,
like a stream we could hold
forever in our hands.

Kyle Coare

If I close my eyes

If I close my eyes,
I'm a beach.
I'm the waves
and the gulls up high.
I'm the sky,
sunlight touching
the ground
like fingers
on a lovers thigh.

When I open them,
I'm a busy waiting room.
A hospital bed, forgotten
in side ward gloom,
nothing feels complete.
No part of me that doesn't ache.
and everything is coated
in big tidal waves of doom.

If I close my eyes
I'm cosy warming dreams.
I'm moonlight teasing
the curtains with a delicate
gentle breeze, rustling them
to let some air in to breathe.
I'm a lover walking towards
a grand castle of light,
where the queen of time
sits awaiting my sight.

If I open them
I'm alone again,
just bright lights
peering directly
at the thoughts
in my head...

Oh, please don't read
these thoughts, I scream.
I don't want you
to witness my dreams,
or see me in this state.
You may see the girl
with luscious hair,
eyes that sing
so beautifully
and a smile that
pulls the stars
from the sky
and reignites
the incandescence
that burns so bright.
You may see her
as she walks across my beach
at midnight
bathing in the moonlight
and you may realise
that she looks just like you.
So please don't read my thoughts,
not whilst I'm here
vulnerable
with nowhere to hide.

Sombre son

See that silver star twinkling,
the one that glows so bright,
the one I speak to alone at night,
pulsing somewhere
light years away
beaming in the cosmic sky.
Silent tears slowly dry,
but memories never die,
giving me the strength
to face every savage day.
So, like that star
I'll sing in joyfully tone,
but inside
I'll be a sombre sun,
burning when
I am alone.

I see you there,
in the vast expanse.
In the refreshing waters,
in the renourished plants.
The soil,
fertile and growing,
vibrant fields flowing
in the gentle winds
you are blowing,
and on this sea
of flower-born memory,
I'll be the boat rowing along,
singing a joyful sailing song,
but inside I'll always be
your sombre son.

The November chill
can drop like a brick,
making icicle tears
spear your heart so quick.
Each one a flash, a glance
at a day now buried
far away in the distance,
but I'll always remember
the love that warmed through,
like a fire melting
the stalactites of misery,
leaving me
with only pools of memory
to dive into.
For a moment
I'll smile
and believe you are there in the room,
but then I'll see that sparkling star,
beside the shimmering moon,
and I'll sing a joyous song,
but inside
I'll always be your sombre sun,
trying to warm up everyone.

Shallow grave

Spent too long in
this bed-shaped coffin.
No lid, no walls,
but I feel stuck,
confined within.
This shallow grave,
dug into the bed,
clinging memory foam
sparks hollow dreams
in my head.
I don't have energy to move.
My feet have forgotten the groove.
All I can seem to do is watch
the insides of my eyelids droop.

Depression deadening
my expressions.
Face splays out,
like a stray cat
on a hot tarmac
roadside. My smile,
forgotten, feels more like
a lead weight around my lips.
An anvil pulling my jaw
distressingly towards the floor.
A workout just to lift,
an exercise in futility,
trying to make this
disturbing frown shift.

Curled into a ball,
in my squeezed in
little corner
beside the wall.
I make myself,
small.
I see the tear-shaped
smears across my eyes.
Not cried in some time,
but these riverways are
deeply inscribed,
from where
former tears did fall.

Struggling to even
stumble to my feet.
A face full of stubble
in the mirror I greet.
Cold water, flannel,
can't face the heat.
Just need to shock
some sense back
into me.
A splash at a time.
Washing away
day old grime,
but nothing seems
to clean the fog in my mind.

A moment of clarity

That moment of clarity
when you turn out the light,
welcoming the darkness.
That peaceful kiss of night
which lifts and carries me
under the warming
fluffy clouds of white.
You evaporate like mist,
seeking insight in the duvet sanctuary.
The fortress of solitude and bliss.
Away from the bleak frigid bite,
the frosty abyss of winter
and it's boreal freezing spite.

Further into the duvet
you venture. An explorer
seeking further adventure.
You surrender yourself
to the pain alleviating
head to toe warmth.
The world of the sublime,
a world so calm.

You search further afield,
duvet stretching out forever,
spanning ages, years, miles,
aeons of stories all deliciously
sewn together.
You see new tales woven,
old worn-out fables re-stitched.
You see your own storyline
far away in the distance,
being embroidered
with all new words that fit.
Never a single missed stich.

Deep into the blanket world,
so far that your room
is nothing but a distant memory.
Through the fantasy forests
full of fallen leaves,
a place to rest if you so please.
Beyond the power and magic
of the soothing seas,
into the world of tranquillity,
where silence lives, thrives and
soundlessly breathes.
Even the echoes of footsteps
are softened by the lush grass.
Not a single noise shall pass.

A space completely at ease,
surrounded by the midnight scents
of the freshest trees,
flowers that only stir at night,
there to perfume the air
whilst the moon is sharing
her magic light, then faded
into an echo of what will be when
dawn cracks the sky in two.

Pollution is just an outside memory,
here in the quilted palace of dreams.
A world of peacefully darkness
where your mind can truly sing,
it can be free to explore the mysteries,
just block out the daily worries,
those wretched noises in your head.
Focus on the spaces
in-between
the duvet and your bed.

Kyle Coare

The smirking silence

The eerily smirking silence
gets broken every few seconds
by the shrill sound.
Metallic blade grating
against brickwork pathway.
The sound says that *HE* is working.
Death hangs his head heavily in the air,
but his work here is never done.
Always another someone.
Always another
mothers daughter or son.
His shift goes on.
And on.
And on.

The lights change after dark,
a grimace from a smirk.
These are the hours
where the beasts lurk.
Looking for those
that are ripened by time,
or the wrinkling weariness,
the universal pen running out of lines.
These are the hours
of which we don't talk,
they don't sit on clocks,
they don't stand in wait.
They just pounce on you
when the human discerned hour is late.
But here
these times
are never done,
these dreaded hours tick slowly on.
And on.
And on.

The clinging scent,
decay and pain.
Tastes like the gasses
from the grimmest
bowels of hell.
It grips the back of your throat
like a leech
sucking your life,
from within its
lung-shaped prison cells.
But these smells never fade,
they pervade the brain.
Invading. An insane army
that always marches on.
And on.
And on.

Phantom rivers of light

I want to kiss
the dark void,
knowing that my lips
will connect
with your soft head.
Feel your warmth,
as we lay
shipwrecked
on this desert island bed.

Barely visible
through the dark,
just the moonlight
upon skin.
Etched outlines
over which
fingertips embark,
across the stark
canvas of night.
Lines that mesmerise.
I'm drawn to memorise,
by painting them every
day and night,
into the dawning
drawing pad of my mind.

Breath races at a heightened pace
as I trace the moonlight
which enlightens your face,
as you lay in the darkness
beside me. The lapping waves
of the sea or butterflies awakened
deep in the belly, trying to break free.

All I see are
imaginary palm trees
shimmering out of view,
and you,
those lines
of perfection,
phantom rivers of light,
solid under fingertips of love,
that the night-time moon above
has deemed in need of projection,
and who am I to question?
When I'm sinking into
the ocean of your affection.

And as the sunlight
starts to glow
I'll be even more dazzled,
by the sight
so many miles below.
In this bed, once an island
on an empty ocean,
now a glowing landscape,
a temple of emotion.
And you lay beside me here,
no longer just outlines,
whole landscapes appear,
becoming more defined,
and the image
is divine.
I want to spend eternity
tracing every line.

Nectar from a tree

The sound
of snow thawing.
Still. Silent.
Or is it?
If you listen
to the pull of the atoms,
they fizzle, with excitement.
Bubbling over like a frothy drink
shaken to the edge of an explosive brink.
Like school children on a bus,
given too much sugar. The can
explodes in a blink. A volcanic splash
of gushing, fizzing energy rushes past.
The sparks and cracks of the universe
putting in one final gasp
before it gives up and snaps.

You hear the slurps and pops.
The splashes as the crashing
ice palace cascades.
Mini avalanches
grinding against stone
towards the ground
like a million
pounding
feet, a sound
like thunder
marching home
or gunfire tearing
the sky in two.

It's like static
buzzing through a universe of sound.
Spoken almost secretly.
Just a crackle, a glitch,
but turn to the channel and tune
it a bit, twist your head
to catch the frequency
and you may get a clearer view.
We are all vibrations of this grand,
stirring cosmic stew.
No matter how far and wide,
the whispered words sometimes creep through.

Sometimes the sounds do go silent,
and I hear only you.
Your breath passing through your lips,
into the atmosphere where it dances and slips,
flipping and tripping with the atoms,
before landing on my cheek to plant me a kiss.

And your voice
like flowing nectar from a tree,
takes my body, drags me closer to happiness
than anything
I could ever construct, purchase or construe.
Every hair stands on end
trying to get closer to you,
to be one of the few
to be touched by your sweet sound
as it flows through.
Every goosebump comes out to witness.
They can't resist it,
like a siren song, that voice,
the pull of an ocean,
and we can only ever drown
in those sounds when we hear them come.

My hapless heart

As you lay,
sprawled out
across my dreams.
My hapless heart
tripped and fell
madly, deeply over you.
As the world slipped
past in slow motion,
it let out a startled scream,
which bounced from the walls
of this discarded seashell.
Where now he sits,
forever part of the
ocean dream swell.

If you lift it to your ears,
you will hear a call.
As sure as a seashore
would normally appear,
instead, you will hear
a heartbeat.
As all around you
silence will fall.
No hum, no numbing
sounds.
Just the beat of my heart,
timing its thuds
along with the stars
silent twinkling chimes.

As you meander
like a river
through my dream,
I'll be there
in the soft ripples
of a stream,
like sauce cuddling
the finest ice cream.
I'll be the feather
that floats on the breeze,
landing soundlessly at your feet,
fingers teasing
the softest of skin.
I'll be the birdsong
that you hear,
singing gentle lullabies
to the leaves,
wishing the moonlight
a sweet night, as she seals
our dreams with a kiss.

Seeking answers to questions unknown

We travelled as far
as we could.
First, by ship,
then on foot.
We walked the earth,
every inch
that stood.
From the
deepest chasms
to the highest mountains.
We kept going.
Searching.
Seeking
Something
we couldn't
quite fathom.

Earth exhausted
we took our pursuit to the stars,
first into orbit
then to the moon and mars.
We took our time
devouring the surfaces,
scouring the lands.
Seeking.
Searching
for some long-forgotten question
that slipped like water through
the fingers of our hands.

We travelled
as far as we could.
A million stars. A billion.
A trillion different worlds
all like ours.
To the absolute limit
of space, where even infinity
has had to give up the pace,
and sat still
clicking copy and paste.
Yet still it was eluding us.
The question. The answers.
The meaning.
Then we sat and looked
into each other's eyes, quizzically.
Therein grew another feeling.

A silent cry. A solitary tear drop.
All those years searching. Seeking.
Ever expanding spaces,
reaching for something untouchable,
and the answer was there all along.
It's the one lesson we should be teaching.
Love.
The answer
was always love.
Not the stars above,
or the lands below,
nor the vast oceans that flow,
but the light that glows
in the eyes of someone
you can't bear to let go.

Snoozed

I wish to see you
in my deepest dreams,
but it appears
you must be awake.
The bridge across
the sleep lake
has been sheared,
too many holes
have appeared
to get across it safe.
I hope you are
not gripped by fear,
or that darkness
isn't holding you near.
I miss you
when you don't appear,
when my dreams are shaded
in faded, melancholic, metallic blue.
I miss you so very dear, it's true.

The bed feels all wrong,
like a lullaby
with lyrics to
a different song.
This blanket of night
isn't holding me right,
it doesn't feel
like your arms
gripping me tight.
Not warming me like it should.
I'm just left here alone,
ice crystals chilling my blood.

The duvet of dreams,
not as comforting
as it usually seems,
your body heat
is missing,
and it appears
the fabric is
frayed at the seams.
The mattress is lumpy,
I'm confused
by this bumpy ground.
I feel so alone
when I walk through
my dreams
and you are not around.

I wish to sleep
but it seems every time
I close my eyes
I'm missing
that second heartbeat,
like ships passing on the tide,
we must be out of sync tonight.
Our clocks on the blink,
mine is alarming me,
whilst yours is a calming sea.
My alarm blares through,
as you are away on a dream cruise.
My storm comes crashing
whilst your gentle breeze
is snoozed.

Kyle Coare

Memories in the clockface

I remember days
beside the sweetest tides.
Fairground rides and fantasy.
Our escape boat getaway
sailing on that steady sea.
Those worn steps
to the highest peaks.
A clock creaking.
Hours unspoken,
words we thought
we'd never speak.
Minutes we never
thought we'd seek.

I remember
ice cream drizzles
dripping
on sizzling
sands,
as we locked eyes
and clasped tightly
our hands.
Never
wanting
to let go
of these seconds
as they slip
steadily
across
the face
of time.

I remember
kisses
taking my
breathe,
giving it to you,
to store
forever
in reserve.
To preserve
the time
we had
to share.
I remember
your hair,
touching my face,
teasing
a feathery embrace.

I remember
standing
in sunsets,
as the moon
rises.
I can
never forget,
the reflection
in your irises.
Even though
none of this
has happened
yet.

A message in a kiss

I yearn
to be beside
you.
Feeling the earth
slowly turn
on its axis,
through
the galactic mist,
as the stars
slowly burn.
Sprinkling us in
star dust wishes.
A message
in a kiss.

I crave
for my heartbeat
to send rippling
waves.
Churning
the ground,
ploughing
a pathway,
from my feet
to yours.

And on the
breath of
song,
I long for
my tears to give
to that canyon,
a belief
in love so pure.

On the kisses we set free,
upon winds that speak.
Blown to the air to reach
frozen cheeks.
I will sail within my boat,
my soul catching the breeze.
To carry me, on these waves.
To land upon your remote island.
To be stood upon those banks,
where only true love gets to reach.

I will fill
a waterway,
with crystal beads,
seeding light into rainbow fields,
distilling that water
into a drink
to pour out
for everyone,
so, they can taste
loves power
so pure.

No matter how
many miles long
the journey from my
shore to yours,
one day I'll surely
arrive at your door,
to share
a message
in a kiss.
A memory
we can hold
forever in bliss.

Kyle Coare

Midnight drapes

Midnight unbuttons her velvet gown,
drops it flowing to the ground.
Stars fizzle and burn,
planets spin and turn.
She stands before me now,
exquisite in moonlit delicate sheets,
draping her shape, so precious and sweet.
I struggle to breathe, any breath may cause
this scene to evaporate,
becoming the death of a dream,
and I want to be a bringer of life.
So, I hold on tight to the thought of you,
the bearer of light guiding us
through this perfect night.

Midnight lakes shimmer,
I see them beyond
my wide-eyed view.
Beauty glimmers
beneath the starlight.
A striking silhouette of you.
Candle constellations
float on this picturesque lake.
Rowboat takes me so far away
from the grim, dingy city,
to a faraway fantasy place,
which sits imitating
your most beautiful face.
I cling on awaiting
where the water will take me,
like a heavenly painting
in a picture book dream.

I see midnight outtakes.
The moments
that most walk past,
not noticing the outlines traced,
where long forgotten footprints
of history have paced.
Fierce red lips that
shine so bright
and taste like forever
in this blink of a life.
The momentous smiles
that you bring to the table.
Eyes of blinding white
that make the moon
just a secondary character
in this ongoing fable.

I see midnight
draped in moonlight.
Now her gown is gone
and her beauty
stands alone, no protection,
just this perfect projection,
throughout my dream insight.
That smile, those eyes,
and the magic dust words and voice
that I grab hold of tight
in a bubble of hope,
trust and love,
to whisk away the night.

Kyle Coare

Circumnavigating snow globes

In dreams
I travel back in time,
to places that I visited long before,
but now the outlines have changed,
the ground magical,
landscapes, fascinating.
A past day,
where nothing happened
now turns into a gateway
to a whole new mystical reality.
I explore the different sides of me,
as a viewer like I'm stood outside
peering through a window
watching a tv screen.
It's all a bit askew,
but it helps me get through
those mixed-up moments of daylight
when I'm caught in a stew.

In dreams
I look to other worlds gyrating
as they dance through gravity fields,
complete with raggedy straw scarecrows.
I try to navigate, but my mind
is somewhere else
circumnavigating snow globes
in a frozen state.
Nothing much makes any sense.
It's so complex trying to contemplate
the incomprehensibly dense static
of a space made of magic.

As I fly through iris fields
trying to see inside,
I see planets evolve
in the blink of an eye,
I look deep inside ours,
to decipher meaning
to riddles I've strived
to answer all of my life.
I witness the birth of planets,
the explosion of stars.
The expansion of gasses,
as space zips away from us.
I see thousands of years of history
played in reverse, to a majestic
round of applause, in a theatre surrounded
by a million versions of me,
stretching into infinity asking for an encore.

In dreams I reminisce
about moments that never exist.
That kiss, that last dance
on a shoreside in bliss.
Those wondrous lips.
Seeking release
and finding pleasure
within the soft embrace
and the delicate pressure.
The wave of a heartbeat,
rhythmically beating one word.

Love.

And I realise that this.
This is the only answer
I was ever really searching for.

Let go of a feeling

Do I just let go of a feeling?
In between fleeting moments
of wonder I fear so much.
This awful being cuts me apart
with just a word, disconnects my life support
when she says I'm never going to be enough.
I should walk away, take the highway,
but it's so much easier to stay.

How can you turn off a thought?
It's not like a light switch
that you can flick, a button to click
or a gear stick you can shift to reverse.
It's a part of your life,
even though it makes you feel worse.
I know I should pull the plug
but it's like a drug. One drag and your hooked,
and I injected the whole lot into my blood.

How can you close that door in your head?
The one she sits behind to keep you on edge,
twiddling her fingers and snarling away,
just waiting impatiently for you to pass her way.
The door she wedged open to watch
the tears fall like weights of lead.
You can't evict a person
from the space in your head.
You can't just close your eyes,
soaked and tear lined, she lurks inside.
I know I should cut my losses
but I know what the cost is,
when the shakes get too much,
she is always first in touch
to try to stop it.

Do you try to seek escape,
leap into a river deep?
Or a disturbed, distorted sleep.
Let the knives cut you,
those piercing eyes.
The vicious lies,
the insistent put down lines.
Do you fall for drugs or drink,
to push you to the brink?
Oblivion is such a sweet retreat.
I know I should open my eyes,
but tears cried are like
threads sewing them tight.
Blinded by the briefest hint of light,
I've become so used to the dark
of another lonely night.

Comatose hope
lost in shrub land.
I took too high a dose.
Can feel the thoughts clawing,
skin crawling.
My brain itches.
Just a heart contained
within a shell of nervous twitches.
I know I should clear my mind,
but I lost the pathway so far behind.
And now the night is here
It's too dark to find, I feel blind.
Trees are rooting in my head
need to find a clearing
in this forest of dread.

Music is

Music is
the emotion we feel.
The adrenaline that
rushes the blood,
flooding our heads,
flooring us when love
walks through the door.
When we feel like a flower bed.
It is the high
when we see a smile
and sounds ring in your mind.
A song, playing on repeat,
as you stand shuffling your feet.
Scared that your heart
won't ever hit the same beat again.

Music is the rush,
the pounding rhythm
of your heart at the first touch.
The sudden onsct anticipation,
this new construct, a creation
of something
indescribable.

Love.

Music is
trying to explain
this unexplainable feeling,
when it's just as mysterious
as the wonders
of space up above.

Music is lust.
That passion which ignites inside,
could burn down barriers a mile wide.
Music takes you flying around the world,
knowing that in the songs
the world will protect you
all the way back home.
Music is hope,
the note that plays to say
don't give up,
tomorrow is on its way.

Music is love.
Something we can't hide,
though sometimes we try,
it's there in our songs
painted on in sky-high lights
of the most luminous neon shine.
In every stutter we speak,
every flutter, a heartbeat
trying to break free, to reach out.
Every word we speak, a love letter,
formed from all the words
we missed out, hidden and twisted
into an invisible canvas
of words crossed out,
that only the right ears
can ever hear aloud.

Glittery butterflies

On that
voiceless
silent night,
something
was planted,
deep inside.

A thought.

Caught on a
breath of wind,
to become part
of my
dreams.

Like
a seedling,
needing
to be
entrenchcd
deep in
this
muddy soul.

It would need
feeding,
nourishment
to aid
its journey
of healing,
to rebuild
this broken
shell
into something
whole.

That distant
twilight
under silver
spotlight,
I heard
a whisper.
Delicately
delivered
from the sweetest
honey drenched lips.
Just a message.
To hold
tightly
to every
word sent
on the waves
of moonlight.
They will help
to put things right.

The kiss of life sent,
just sat awaiting
its delivery,
a feeling,
glittery butterflies
making my insides
feel jittery,
skin tingling,
shivery.
And I sit
here on
the periphery,
in gradual
recovery.

Kyle Coare

Disassociated

A chill shiver
disturbs the dead night.
Love not sat in the sky,
hope not twinkling bright.
Just the ink blot imagery
projecting bad thoughts
and strained memory
through the ever-expanding
eerie light.

Your spirit walks on.
Unaware that your body
left so long ago. It took flight,
floated away along a pathway
paved with night.
Lungs no longer breathing air.
Heart buried in an unmarked grave.
Where it is you are unaware.
Yesterday remains just a faded wave,
a recollection that no longer stands
where that shoreline meets the day.

Consciousness shivers
in and out of the shimmering air.
Body conspicuous in its absence.
Yet still ice spills everywhere
that your stamped footprints
should appear.
Murkiness fills every inch
of misty atmosphere,
encircling your wavy form.
Disassociated from everything.
You think,
is this now the norm?

Body nowhere
to be seen.
Nobody sees
where you've been,
no body
sits where
you search
through the
glassy sheen.
A glossy red smear
on yesterday.
The gossamer thread
on this reality
starts to tear.
Broken thoughts
smash through
your head.
Floating along.
Alone.
Disassociated.

*Is this what
it feels like
to be dead?*

Paradise with moonlight guide

You show me paradise
when my view of reality
begins to thin.
Along the corners of the ordinary,
across the edges of the divine,
you show me your brown eyes.
Every blended colour pulsating
whilst this world slowly spins.
So many gold mine sunsets
lined within.

You show me
paper fragments of eternal storylines,
pages tinted with the colour of time.
The handwriting of the divine,
sublime lines written in rhyme.
You take me
to word riverways
into which I'd gladly dive,
to swim by your side
in this perfect world that you abide.
A queen of light, princess of midnight.
Goddess of moonlight,
I want to stay by your side.

You show me reasons to smile,
you show me acres and miles,
luxury satin sheet sunsets
through which I'd glide
on the wings
of golden birds.
You show me
your smile
and I feel so alive.

You share with me
insight and I dream.
You share starlight
and I see the glorious
universe shifting between.
You feed my eyes
the wonder
of the eternally blinking
cosmic lights.
You complete
my days,
so that the night
is ours.

I stare
into twilight
and daydream
about your moonlight,
keeping me
company
for the rest
of my life.

Moss upon a stone

Love can make you weak,
cause you to weep
tears of loss.
Years gone,
but at what cost?

It can leave you feeling
like moss upon a stone.
Growing stale, fearing you've failed.
You try to atone,
for crimes, not committed,
but you can't repair time
or something you didn't break,
no matter how
the claim is reshaped.

Love can steal
your unique mentality.
Morphing you
into a clone, a sheep,
so desperate to hear
the way she bleats,
you miss the darkness
below the eerie undertones.
You sink into obscurity,
thinking only in terms of sentimentality.
She wouldn't hurt me on purpose,
she is trying to make us work.
Of course, all this does is send
your thoughts off course.
But love insists that this
is what works best for you.
So, you follow the story through,
even if the segments,
when unpeeled, feel unreal
or completely untrue.

Love bites
on cold lonely nights.
when the old you
comes over to stay.
It absorbs all light,
like the blackest paint
in a sealed-tight room.
It chokes with reminders
of that stale perfume.
A love-gas chamber
to fill with gloom.

Love leaves you
floundering.
A fish in the desert heat.
Love makes it harder to trust,
as your old, unbeating,
steely heart crumbles
into red dust flakes,
as years of rust shakes free.

Love can make you weep,
as the words seep into your skull,
the embodiment of the anti-muse
will try to lull your mood,
to cull your thoughts
before they come to you.
Slurping on your creative juices,
until a withered husk
is all you are reduced to.

Kyle Coare

Hole into my heart

That look burned
a lip shaped hole
into my heart.
A fiery kiss
sizzling the raw muscle
until it is charred
and tenderly tearing apart.
The beating muscle
in my chest, so rarely used,
barely up to the test,
too often abused,
but I knew that my life was
forever changed because I'd met you.

That look, a wink,
saying I see you
and you see me
I see below the mask you use
and you see the truth
in the words I choose.
I see that look
and the way it brings
with it a friend. The little grin,
that starts to form from nothing.
Making the eyes infuse
with dancing delight,
and from that moment
to deny was no use,
I wanted to share in that magic light.
I just hoped it wasn't a burning fuse.

And I'm falling.
So fast,
I'm down in a pit,
into hell I have been cast.
This seemingly
endless hole
down which I hurtle,
knowing that these
thoughts are not fertile.
They can't be allowed to show.
The seeds are not to be sown,
not to become a field
upon which that blossom can grow,
from which we can watch
the clouds gently billow.

I see that look
and all these thoughts
fall away from me.
Deep in the pit,
but I am slowly
being raised out of it.
Those thoughts
will linger at the bottom,
and I will often
return to revisit.
Wondering if my
silence was golden,
or a chance of happiness,
forever stolen.

Deliver me

Deliver me
your emotions,
handwritten
in ocean blue ink.
I'll rip apart
the envelope,
and into those
words I'll sink.
Letters float past
as I go deeper
into briny memories.
Sky ahead overcast
as the stormy sensation
enters me.

Let me delve
into your fervent mind.
Dive through
deep-water words
left behind.
I want to soak
in your pain,
be a servant to guide
through the driving rains.
To unblur visions,
I'll help you clean the windows
of hurt and shame,
making the outlines more defined,
to show, you are not always to blame.
I want to read between the lines,
find the parts you were
too scared to impart.
To help you see the signs
pointing the way
to your heart.

I'll peer
at your mind designs,
find memories inside.
Wander through
your gardens of reminiscence
and find reminders inside,
post it notes
pointing out memories, arrows float
showing more stories inside.

Those never-ending images,
appearing ever deeper you look,
a new vision leaps out
taking you further into
the world you overlook.
The magnified emotions
ripple like tidal surges
as all the memories converge
on every page of an unopened book.

Flowerbeds

Fingers slide through
your dark black hair,
like vines entwining
to become one
interwoven dream.

Our petal clothing
dropping, like a leaf
from a book of mystery,
to share the magical escapades
of our endless story.

As eyes gaze into mine,
in a dream scene springtide,
we slip into another world,
we stretch out
across flowerbeds,
two new buds feeling
the air for the very first time.

The duvet shaped
like a rose petal's
perfect form,
holding us close
like a sleeping bag.
Skin against soft skin,
safe and warm.
Luxuriously watching time
slowly crawl.
We have all the time.
We let the rest of our petals fall.

In this bed of roses,
no thorns, just
perfumed beauty.

Where the sun
earlier shone down,
now the moons
beaming light
lazily grazes
upon the ground.

The interwoven
branches
dance together
in her ethereal
stage light.
Hands held tight,
as the stems
become twirling vines,
strong in all weather,
holding together the night.

Roots meld,
as the stems
become one
in a dream
of loving
forevers
we would
outshine the sun.

Numbed

Numbed by
days numbered,
I slept through
my best years
in a deep
slumber.
I fought monsters
in dreams,
swam in oceans
and deep seas,
but never
left a mark,
a part of me
for the world
to see.

Troubled times
tumble by
in a heartbeat
of double lines
and slowing
vital signs.
I fought demons
in my head,
and they won
so many fights.
Endless nights
left in despair,
and all I got
in return were
new scars to bare.

Off the scale,
the shakes rumble forth,
an emotional earthquake
shaking somewhere deep inside.
Hit the brakes. We are gonna collide!
I can't think straight,
all I can do is lay here and cry.
Just staring into
the ever-calling oblivion,
nothing to say as a reply.

This is a new low,
so much deeper than I usually go.
All new places to explore,
new taunts thrown at my head,
the haunting whispers from before
now shouts instead.
Put downs and slights, frightening insights.
Lightning quick replies
to make me quiver in dread,
and I have nothing to give,
no witty reply,
I'm just here trying
my hardest to survive.

Tearful eyes,
remind me of lost lives.
Signs flickering like static sighs,
whispering of long-lost goodbyes.
Bulbs blowing out
like candles in a breeze,
the flames dance
but soon they always leave.
I am left here to try to repair
the damage caused
by this smoky air.

Out of sight, out of mind

The dead stay silent.
It's supposed to be
the one great constant.
Death comes for us all,
rich or poor,
but sometimes
the dead don't
get the memo.
They sometimes
forget to take
the unearthly door.

Through those lonesome hours
their screams violently echo.

Out of sight, out of mind.
Words that are not true,
ghostly footsteps creep through
the darkness crawling behind.
Out of sight, out of mind.
Not so true when the sound
of chattering is all that echoes,
singing throughout the night.
Out of sight, out of mind.
Not when the night-time
feels so hollow,
not sleepy,
not when the sound
of shallow breathing
does follow.

The dead shouldn't
be seen or heard.
They shouldn't
walk the earth,
or so we are
led to believe.

Sometimes the soul
doesn't want to leave.

It festers in the world
just beneath ours,
caught in the
dimensional scars
of this ripped, torn
universe of
shattered hearts.
It lingers
in the corners
of sleepy eyes,
where shadows
can menacingly
slip by.

Most of the time
you won't notice
their visage
floating there,
but then
other nights
are a waking
nightmare.

Made of starlight

I stand here
watching
the night.
The exquisite stars
painting pictures
on the
canvas
of the sky,
but through
their lustful
light,
I see a
different
image
blurring across
my eyes.
Not twisting
serpents
of the
heavens above,
nor ships
made of cloud vapour
that sail
overhead,
instead
I see the stars
blur and bend,
twisting,
transforming,
into a vision
of you.
A beauty
made of starlight.
A beauty too good
to be true.

I wonder
are you
looking up
at them too?

Are they
melting
into a whole
new view?

Do you see
what I see?

Or does your sky
only contain images of
worlds that can never be?

Do your images
contain me?

Do I stand longingly
looking out at you?

Are you longingly
looking up
at me too?

Question not

I try to question not
from whence they came.
I don't wish to enflame
the poetry overlords,
whose words splash
into my brain, like puddles
after a stormy rain.

Who am I to try to second guess
the who, whats, wheres and whys?

I just thank them
for putting their trust in me,
to take their words
and manipulate them
so delicately,
to place into these
pages of mine.

Sometimes the words
are just there, floating
before my eyes,
like white dandelion puffballs
catching the light
as they blow across
the wispy sky.

Who am I to ignore
these words?

They are given to me,
to pull apart
then replant them
in the depths of my heart.

I try to just accept that words
will invade my dreams.

I'll be walking
in some mystic
magical scene,
and a waterfall
of sentences will pour
from the lined pathway
towards the everlasting stream.
I'll dunk my hands in deep
and pull out as many as I can find,
before I wake from my sleep
and write them down,
before they can vanish
from my mind.

Who am I to neglect
the constant sound of words?

I take every opportunity
afforded to me
to take these words
and create something
equally as beautiful
as the worlds
from which
these words
originate.

Who am I to reject
the poetry god's gifts to me?

Kyle Coare

Years of his returning

Sleepy eyes sloop off,
seeking respite
in the shadows
of his frowning
upside down smile.
Sea mist breeze
moistening
the dry skin beneath,
or is that the tears
in which he doesn't
want to believe?

Over him falls
a wintery haze
of reminiscence.
With persistence
it springs into view,
as clear as day,
like a kiss that tingles
for a second, then slowly
fades back away from you.

Now just a part
of the scenery.
The sea mist
blowing gales freely.
The moistness
threatens
to overpower
as it rolls down
his already
saturated cheek.

He sees
on the seat
beside him,
a feint scrawl,
etched by two
teenage hearts
so many summers
before.
A pull on his heart,
like the waves ripping apart,
causes more
moistness to release.
Glistening as it falls
gently from his chin.

Thoughts locked
deep inside.
Words from which
he cannot hide.
Words he can't form into voice.
Looks over at the countryside,
then back at the sea view.
I miss you. Love was a song
and he didn't know how to dance.
Two left feet, so instead he just stands
watching those seaside sands,
where so often a flood of tears lands,
beside the rockpools,
that have formed
over years of his returning.

Lollipop skies of life

Just a lick
of light
slinking through
the candy floss
clouds sat teasing
the caramel glass horizon.

We walk under
these sweet delights
You and I.
To taste the lollipop
skies of life.
So far apart,
but the
same skies
fill our eyes.

Sherbert fantasy landmarks
tingling into view,
the fizzle of electricity,
creating goosebumps
like a field upon skin
coated in the finest mist of dew.
Your fields, so far away,
would work so perfect
laying next to mine,
a patchwork display
playing over
a countryside
seen from
lemon drizzle
skies.

As night
transpires,
to fill
minds
with lust,
listless thoughts
explore
loves
sugar dust.
The silver wrapped
moon
shines across
the chocolate
wrapper blue.
Stunningly it all combusts,
stirring the paint
of this room.
Making
the colours
meld,
dancing,
swirling through.

As we caress and kiss
completely ignoring the view.

Kyle Coare

Heart on my sleeve

Heart on my sleeve.
It was stuck
deep in my throat.
Making me choke.
Words wouldn't pass,
they made me gasp,
grasping for air.
Made me feel
lightheaded and weak
Now it's on my sleeve.
Leaving me free to speak.

I etch my words
onto that heart
Every emotion taken
and burned
into every beating part.
The hurt
that tears a hole
in the centre,
I fastened loosely
back together
with the happiness
I find in the moments
I can remember.

Sticking plasters and adhesive tape.
Bandages hold it all in shape.
Frayed strands of string,
sewn deep, so that the ends don't tether.
I bind it to keep the pieces held tightly together.
Afraid it may fail to start,
or I may lose a part
if it tries to beat too strongly,
this stitched up heart.

For far too long I lost my way.
So now I hang a compass from my heart,
always points my direction home.
When I'm lost, alone or my world
is slowly falling apart. I always know
the direction to scrawl upon my chart.

I take words like strength, resolve.
and I force them back in.
Turning them around my mouth
until I can feel every brittle edge.
Until each letter shard is mixed
with my blood. They become my food.
My saviour in this world of hunger.

I take feelings of hurt
and put them
where they belong.
In a prison
of my own creation,
incarcerated
with hate and anger
that grows like a cancer.
I visit them sometimes,
to give introspection
until they have withered
into shadows
of their former selves.

Kyle Coare

Human stew

First you pour
a few splashes of love,
then sprinkle a dash of hope
in a flowing motion
from above.
Add some finely chopped
ambitions,
be sure to dice them thin.
Take a pinch of imagination
and stir it all in,
just for safe measures
add another pinch.
Now the base
should be sizzling.

Add the juice
of the sweet
sun-wisened fruit of life,
matured over time
to provide
the perfect bite.
This will give bursts
of sweet memories,
making your dish
a joy to eat.
Now taste the sauce,
add a few fresh smiles,
and the odd choice joke,
then blend in a particular
loved song of yours.

Now to prepare
the meat of a story.
Cut it into chunks,
now season with a few
sprigs of life history.
Dust with flowers
to perfume every anecdote.
Add this all to the base
and let it brown off perfectly.

Take some time to reminisce.
Find that first kiss and splash
a drop or two, this will leave the stew
glistening. Don't worry if the pot
makes a hiss or starts sizzling,
those delicate moments of bliss
will start to spread through the liquid.
Bubbles popping, bursting
to give mouthfuls of joy.

Now add the stock of words
from your pantry store.
Find any roots of celebrations
you enjoyed. Stir them in.
Add pulses of every heartbeat
you have ever felt raising,
add some tears to season the stew.
Now let it simmer, watch as the
bubbles shimmer across the surface,
like reflective moments
of a life well lived.
Once the sauce has reduced,
ladle from the pan
and then you have
the perfect taste of a human.

Used

You used to smile, a glowing halo.
Fun seeking in the warm flow
of summer evenings and day glow.
I'm not sure when the colours flipped
from neon to noir, when the glow faded
into a singular star sat in a sky so vast.

Was it when his words turned on you?
Ganging up, blaming you,
making you feel uncomfortable
in your own skin. Covering up
to become just a clone of him.

You used to paint such fluffy borders
around everything. Your brushstrokes
would bristle with beauty. They would paint;
big and bold, or precise and pretty.
I'm not sure when the pictures became gritty.
When the thorns and thistles blew in,
like pity held by the whistling wind.

Was it when he bruised your frame?
Always someplace out of view.
So, nobody knew. Was it the purple
and yellow paintings too awful to view,
stains, he rained down on you?

You used to draw pretty pink hearts.
Handwriting playing over the page,
words danced like microscopic ants.
Every dot would be a smile,
every word a synonym for good times.
I don't remember when dancing words became
a scratched scrawl, barking and angry at all,
I don't remember when the hearts fell
like rain from the page, replaced
with only storm clouds and downpour.

Was it when his reign of terror truly began?
Words would froth in a gargled roar
from his soiled slurring lips,
No love to give just those ever-hurtful quips,
dripping like a tap over the beer slops.

You used to be sunlight on life's darkened streets.
You would show shadows the door
and push them through. You used to be
a force of nature. Someone that wouldn't
accept any hurt. I don't remember when
that sunlight got lost from view,
when the skies became increasingly overcast.

Was it when he took what was never his?
When he raised a fist and made a scene,
saying not to resist in a voice that was
almost alien and mean.
When he came home pissed
for the 7th time that week,
reeking of some awful perfume.
Rageful. Was it when
he took what was never his?
He stole the last true heart to exist.

Kyle Coare

Winter day

Frost gnawingly bites
at chilled fingers in spite.
My eyes, now iced over
lakes of sight,
condensation inside,
blinding me to
the beautiful light.
I shiver away the chills,
but they come back
twice as cold, demanding a fight.
My shaking, wakes the birds in the trees,
the trill sound
feels like a drill grinding into teeth.

If it wasn't so cold and my eyes were not
so cloudy, this would be such pretty a scene,
moonlight licking at the iced lake,
like a refreshing sorbet, to keep her palate clean.
Little drifts of lily white, specking everything,
like tiny little fireflies landing at my feet.

Crunchy snowfall. Deep in places.
Angel wings play beside where snowmen call.
Trees sway, holding out branches
with all new icy fingers,
to beacon forth a bit more winter into the day.
Pathways sparkling,
like an upside-down sky,
stars painting the ground
over which we glide.

I step gingerly forward,
icy paths offer little reward to
shattered glass bones if I fall.
So, I edge onwards.
The journey only short,
but time is dawdling forth,
as the cold makes every step
take the time of four.

One foot in front of the other.
Tentative short strides, if I stretch
I could slide, ending on the ground
feeling the pain in my backside
from landing with a howl.

The cold
is numbing now,
my hands
feel like
slabs of meat,
my feet,
need
a source
of heat.
My energy resources
are almost depleted.
Oh, how I wish
I was at home
comfortably warm
and seated,
thinking of you
and your loving heat.

Kyle Coare

Final pages

What if it's bad news?
What if I've used up
all of my good luck?
If the universe says
that's your lot.
What if. What if.
What if.

I've always had
a lot of fight,
but how much
fight is enough?
Are my tanks nearly depleted?
Puddled,
with just a sheen of luck
starting to evaporate away
from the bottom where it once lay.
Do I still have any reserves left?
It's a mystery of which
I don't want to find in a book.

I'd rather not read the final pages,
leave that to the mysterious sages,
I don't want to know dates, times or ages.
I'd rather just float though days
instead of worrying about time
and it's mysterious ways.
Could I just tear away
those closing sheets instead?
Set them aflame
and watch the embers
fly overhead.

I'd rather take in a lungful
of breath every day,
than fear death or whatever it is
that comes our way.
I've always had a good balance
of fight or flight,
but my flight left a long time ago,
from a different boarding gate.
Now I'm starting to feel depleted
and slightly empty
from worrying about fate.

White lilies

Sent back to earth
amongst flourishing white lilies,
to symbolise rebirth.
Cleansed of life's impurities,
to wander
these everlasting fields of eternity.
A place full of wonderous sights.

Sad eyes cry over memories,
reminiscing of stories
forever marked
in the book of time.
A passing of flames
from one smouldering candle,
to a glowing new torch.
Words imparted start
to burst forth,
encasing images
in new frames.

From whence we came,
a universe of endless possibilities,
tree lined lanes,
beside sunset seascapes,
stretching away,
off into the boundless infinity.
Free of earthly deficiencies and
rotten stench of decay.

We return again.
as the new torch
burns fiercely,
until its time comes
to illuminate
the next in line,
to kindle their fire
and keep on burning
those everlasting flames.

This is the cycle of things.
Life briefly sings,
burning brightly,
a midday sun in spring.
Rebirth in motion,
the swirling emotions
of the immense oceans
that we can swim
within eternally.

Thank you for reading.
If you have enjoyed this book
then please leave a review
where purchased.

Peace, Love & Poetry.
Kyle.

https://linktr.ee/wordsandfluff

The Night Watchman
(2019)
ISBN 978-1797484419

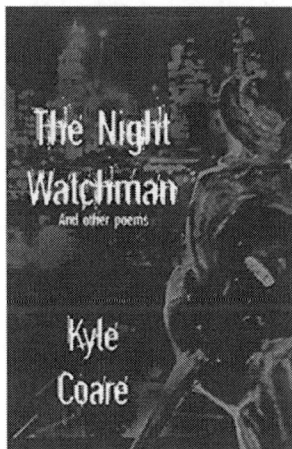

"When day ends, and night falls
When the sun leaves the sky, and darkness calls
The watchman sits, his duty to observe
Protect the dreams, of those who deserve"

This poetry collection takes us on a journey into the murky depths of the night. Down dark alleyways, through disused wastelands.
The beasts are out in force, who will hear our calls?
it will be a long night, but the watchman is looking out for us all.

"The Night Watchman is a thought-provoking carousel of dreams, rage and sympathy all at once. Rebellious but kind-hearted, powerful and fresh. A relevant collection to current problems.
It is an observant and raw book of poems that I would recommend for anybody with a full five stars. If you need proof that poetry is just as vital, if not more vital to literature today than it's ever been, here is proof."
Realistic Poetry International

Seasons
(2019)
ISBN 978-1689340434

"Seasons keep turning, like the hands on a clock
tick tock, the pendulum rocks, as we take stock
days pass, the weather changes on the fly
spring into summer, a gull cries into autumnal skies"

This thought-provoking poetry collection touches subjects ranging from love and loss to addiction and mental health issues.
Taking a tour through the seasons.

"Author Kyle Coare is an exquisite Poet and Word Artist that truly knows how to bring words and the world to life through poetry, and this collection of animated poems is more than proof!
Reader's will experience the rush of each season while traveling through its pages, from summer to winter, to spring to fall, in which we realize just how well life and people mirror the concept and cycle of the seasons and how they change. This book is one of our favourites from the Author. Kyle Coare is both an artist and a poet in this collection, creating specially for the heart, mind, body, and soul. Beautiful work."
Realistic Poetry International

Lone Wolf
(2020)
ISBN 979-8613023912

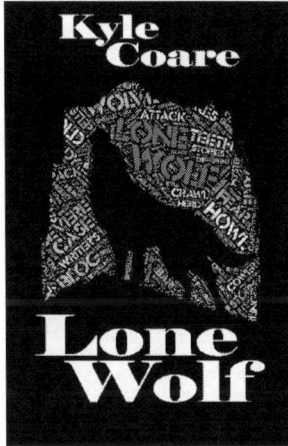

"Wolves howl, they don't cower from the storm
they prowl, they don't crawl or fear the swarm
the lone wolf takes a step from the pack
But don't stand too near, he's ready to attack
Snarling, his teeth glint in the moonlight
The pale spark of hope in the night"

Join the wolf on his path, as he tries to make sense of the world, we
inhabit. Seeking answers in the aftermath of a wrecked planet.
Through the urban wilderness of love and hurt, anxiety and mental
illness. Against the backdrop of an apocalyptic nightmare world,
on the brink of collapse.

*"It is very apparent that many heartfelt efforts went into this book; the
author bares their heart on their sleeve. Thus, we do believe that many
reader's hearts will be equally captivated – just as much as ours were.
the style of writing which is seen within Lone Wolf seems quite unique
and refreshing. Collections like these are a rare breed, and we recom-
mend adding this one to your shelves as soon as possible"*
Realistic Poetry International

Kyle Coare

Headfirst into the storm
(2021)
ISBN 979-8526622288

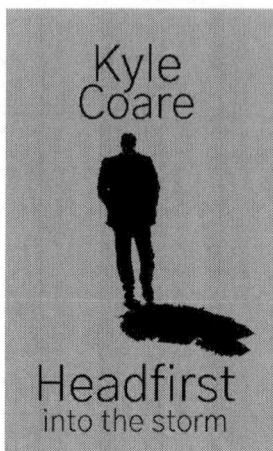

"The rain poured like we had angered the gods
thunder roared lightning struck the brick and stone facades
of the halls that we sat, enclosed inside
nowhere else to hide
we heard the drumming downpour
and we bunkered down fortified"

Feel the cold chill of fear, the icy sting of pain as we run
headfirst into the rain, through a year that never was,
2020 its given name.
Embark on an emotional joyride, let the weather guide
ducking and diving for cover as the driving rains fall
we search for calm trying to find the sunshine after the storm.

"This poetry is rooted solidly to the ground, emotionally reaching down
to hell, but at the same time with moments that can lift the soul.
it could easily be a modern-day Decameron. With 105 poems about life,
mental illness, virus, lockdown, lost love, failed relationships and more
than the odd political and social commentary that lays it on the line.
This is no nonsense, powerful poetry, written to be spoken, not shouted
from a podium, maybe at speaker's corner to get attention or from be-
hind a news desk, because folks what's here is real, it's happening and
we have a responsibility to listen, understand and act."
Carl Butler (Dark Poetry Society)

In Shadows
(2022)
ISBN:979-8448585333

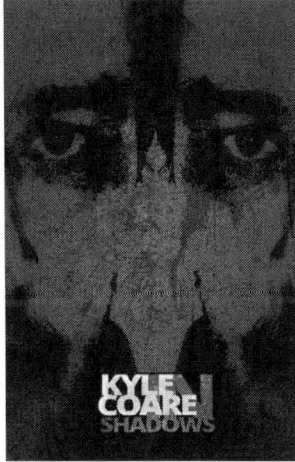

"Something is coming,
its hiding in the dark.
In shadows, it is stalking,
ready to stop your heart"

This poetry collection will take you deep into the bowels
of hell, through its lava filled mouth, where demons howl.
217 pages of horror themed poetry storytelling.
Filled with humour, scares, light and shade.

"Kyle has once again left us spellbound and on the edge of our seats
with this tantalizing collection. The various forms of proses and poetry
take us through the innermost workings of the unexpected ride that is
life. Your mind and soul will dance in grace and reverie, as you move
through its pages. This incredible title is immersive, in every aspect.

"In Shadows" is an exquisitely crafted masterpiece — a micro adventure
that is a delight to experience; don't delay! If you're looking for material
built with genuine care that can offer soft introspection and the thrill of
discovery, this latest treasure from Kyle is the book for you!"
Realistic Poetry International

Torn Pages: Scraps of midnight
(2023)
ISBN: 979-8375840512

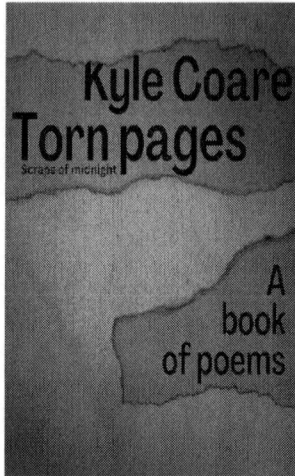

"I bleed internally
from invisible scars.
I want to scream so loudly
I shatter the stars"

Torn Pages is a collection of poems, ripped from the heart, torn from the soul and cut from the mind of poet/author Kyle Coare. Each of the 100+ poems takes you deep into different aspects of life, from love and pain to health and hope. Also touching on struggles with mental health, loss and with society as a whole, whilst always trying to remain playful.

"Any poet this consistent with their skills is destined for greatness!"
Experience the soulful power and journey into the depths of life's emo-
tion through heartfelt words. Feel pain, love, hope and even learn to ac-
cept yourself with this honest & raw collection of poems. Let these pages
become your silent companion as you discover healing and acceptance
with every line.
Torn Pages is absolutely a beautiful piece of work. It's a dreamy, en-
chanting exploration into a broken world. The poems draw you in and
you feel like you are a part of the journey. Torn Pages is definitely worth
every penny, it will stay with us for a long time. We've been reading this
amazing book all day and we can't seem to put it down!!"
Realistic Poetry International

Endless Nightmares
(2023)
ISBN: 979-8394691119

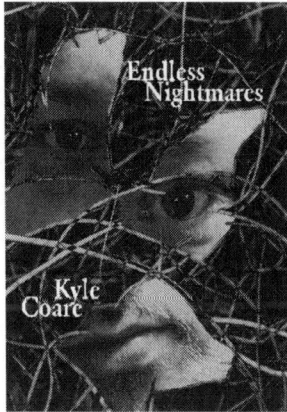

"The shadows warned us,
but we didn't heed their cries"

Kyle Coare brings you more dark tales, more twisted nightmares, in this spiritual successor to In Shadows. Scary visions mired in the shadows. Lurking beasts and crooked wonders. Shady lanes and darkened corners. Apparitions rising from the grave. The shadows warned us, but we didn't hear their cries. The shadows warned us, at the cold dark end of day. The shadows warned us and now the beast is on his way…

"Endless Nightmares is an exceptional, must-read book of poetry
that will give readers nightmares with its vivid and haunting horror-
themed imagery,
a true testament to the author's unparalleled talent, dedication, and skill.
Overall, the book is a heart stopping and addictive experience,
leaving readers excited for what Kyle Coare will create next."
Realistic Poetry International

Carpe Noctem
(2023)
ISBN: 979-8394691119

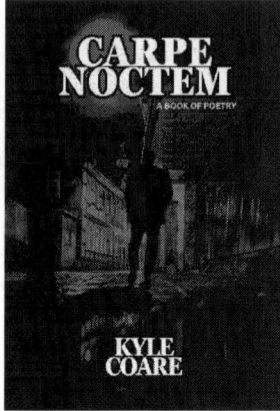

"Carpe Noctem – Seize the night, reclaim the dark as friend"

Into the beauty of dreams, the moonbeams laying fairytale lights over the alleyways and streets. Night has its terrors, but it has love also, so follow as Kyle guides the reader on a journey through the night.

"Kyle Coare has a remarkable talent for tugging at your heartstrings, and in "Carpe Noctem," he explores themes that are lighter in comparison to some of his earlier works. This time around, the poems are brimming with love and hope, delivering an emotional impact that leaves you yearning for more. It's clear that Kyle possesses a raw skill and a deep love for poetry, evident in the vivid imagery and metaphors woven throughout the book.
"Carpe Noctem" stands out as one of his most outstanding works to date His voice is strong, his words powerful and precise, making "Carpe Noctem" a must-read for poetry enthusiasts."
Realistic Poetry International

Poetic Outlaw
(2023)
ISBN: 979-8879303735

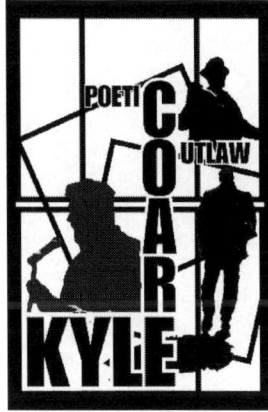

"Don't fear the darkness. The guiding words of the outlaw will shine a light to find us"

A contrasting collection of light and dark, love and hate,
hope and despair, loss, and gain.
So, embrace the darkness,
until a new day envelops you

*"Coare's language is vivid
and evocative, painting pictures
and eliciting strong emotions with each word.
His ability to capture the essence of a moment
or emotion is both relatable and deeply moving.
As a seasoned poet, Coare excels in storytelling,
drawing readers into his narratives
and leaving them yearning for more
as they traverse the pages of his book."*
Realistic Poetry International

Tales from the 44A
(2024)
ISBN: 979-8333917270

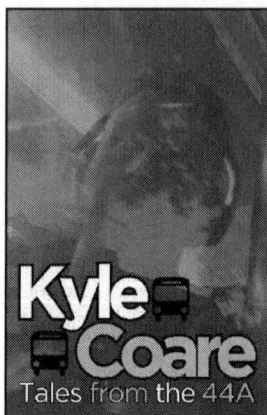

"A flower sits beside the road.
I take a petal, to place inside a book,
an abode for a thought
so long lodged tight,
now unstuck, the words take flight"

"Tales from the 44A offers an emotional and unforgettable journey
into the heart of poetic expression. It stands as a testimony
to the transformative power of art, a refuge for the soul's storms.
With its blend of whimsy, sass, boldness, and clever wordplay,
the collection does not disappoint. Each poem carries an element
of surprise, challenging readers to look at familiar experiences
in new and unexpected ways.

This collection is not just a book of poems;
it's a compelling dive
into the nature of a poet's heart
and the journey of a wordsmith as they find their voice
amidst life's pleasures and perils.

We are confident that Tales from the 44A will become a generational
classic, offering a fresh and tantalizing take on universal concerns. Kyle
Coare's work is truly a masterpiece, one that you will be glad to add to
your collection."
Realistic Poetry International

Stations
(2024)
ISBN: 979-8337919560

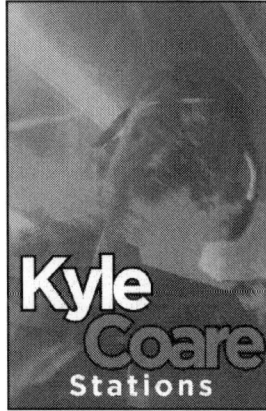

"Feed your dreams into the sea,
Skim those stones of hope, let them bound
Across the waves. I'll wait endlessly
Beneath the reflective shine, I'll wait for all time
For the stone which is mine"

This collection takes readers on a journey through vivid, dreamlike reflections, on recovery, self-awareness, and the complexities of human experience. Combining elements of science fiction, fantasy, and cinematic imagery, Coare crafts poetry that resonates deeply, appealing to readers across multiple genres.

In Stations, Coare's talent for capturing the intricacies of life shines brilliantly. Each poem offers a glimpse into a world both familiar and mysterious, making the collection a powerful choice for anyone seeking insight into the beauty and challenges of existence. It transforms ordinary moments into opportunities for introspection and wonder, creating a deeply emotional and meaningful reading experience.

The collection masterfully balances delicacy and depth, immersing readers in Coare's unique perspective. Themes of peace, emotional awareness, and community echo throughout, exploring the events and choices that shape our lives and futures. From serene observations to moments of haunting unease, Stations delivers a wide range of emotional experiences with creativity and originality.

Realistic Poetry International

Other poets

If you enjoy my work, then please support the poets in your local scene, get along to open mics, buy their books, listen to their words. There really are so many talented writers/performers. Here is just a few that I know and their Instagram handles, please give them a follow.

Aflo.thepoet – Aflo the poet
Awpoetry12 – Amy Walpole
BassieGracie – Gracie
Carolinadailha – Carolina
Pcarmen_poetry_reads – Philip Carmen
Cathirae – Cathi Rae
Courts_ward – Courtney Ward
Mouse_teeth – Nancy Dawkins
Yellow_ellie – Ellie Spirrett
Sharenaleesatti – Sharena Lee Satti
Sammy_Someantics – Sammy Nour
Scottacoe – Scott Coe
Jamesscotthowes – James Scott Howes
Partdalek – Matt Gopsill
Supportyourlocalpoet – Jazmine Cartwright
Bobjimreeves – Rob Reeves
Dannahwritcs – Dannah
Alext_spokennerd – Alex Tyler
Andreamcdowall – Andrea McDowall
Kezzgally – Kerry Gallagher
Arspoeticel – Elena Chamberlain
Nakeishapebody_ - Na-Keisha
J_J_R_B – Jodie
Lauradickinson.creative – Laura Dickinson
Warriorspiritroamingfree – Kamisha Hawkins
Thaughtonpoetry – Ty'rone Haughton

Check out my poetry night,
Get_mouthy_leicester
For lots more poets,
and anyone I've missed I apologise
and will make it up in the next book.

ABOUT THE AUTHOR

Kyle coare is a poet and author from Leicester, England.
His work veers between enchanting beauty and dark nightmares. Bringing
new worlds to life, be they horror landscapes, or dreamy hideaways.
He likes to combine storytelling and poetry, often pointing a spotlight on the
world we inhabit. With some humour and some dark edges but is just as
comfortable writing about love and hope, as he is loss and hurt. His work
can be dark, but through the darkness there is always light.
He has performed at various spoken word events and slams and was the
2022 2funky/Some-Antics slam winner.
He also co-hosts the monthly poetry night Get Mouthy in Leicester.
His work has also featured numerous times on BBC Radio, and Pukaar
magazine.

www.facebook.com/wordsandfluff
Https://linktr.ee/wordsandfluff

Clouds

The body
can feel
so much pain,
but yet,
the right hands
can make
you feel like light,
dancing amongst
the raining
clouds.

Printed in Great Britain
by Amazon